YOUR YOGA EXPERIENCE

52 Comprehensive Lessons for Lifelong Practice

Sandi Greenberg, RYT

December 2012
Kristie —
Enjoy the journey . . . .
Sandi Greenberg

For information about this title or to order other books and/or electronic media, contact the publisher:

Tandu Publications
428 E. Thunderbird #123
Phoenix, AZ 85023
www.NoPlaceLikeOmYoga.com
602-741-2828

Library of Congress Control Number: 2009908693

ISBN: 978-0-9841918-3-3

Printed in the United States of America

Book and Cover design by: 1106 Design

*To my husband Mark and my children
Eytan, Shira and Rod, Lindsey, Edna and David*

Thank you for your love and support

Disclaimer:

Yoga and all forms of physical exertion should be preceded by a doctor's examination and permission. The poses in this book should not be done by inexperienced yoga practitioners without the guidance of a teacher or other experienced practitioner.

The opinions and advice expressed in this book are intended as a guide only. The publisher and author accept no responsibility for any injury or loss sustained as a result of using this book.

Introduction

Yoga has been a huge gift in my life, one that I want to share with as many people as possible. Walls limit the amount of people that can comfortably fit on the floor of my No Place Like Om home yoga studio, but through this book, I hope I can reach far and wide, spreading awareness of the potential for peace of mind and happiness that can be accessed through the philosophy and application of yoga. After all, that's what yoga is about.

When contemplating retirement from my decades as an English teacher, both in Israel and in the U.S., I realized that the natural new path arising for me would be a combination of my experience and skills as a teacher along with my desire to share the richness of all I've found yoga to offer. After preparing in a life-changing 500-hour certification course, I began to teach my own yoga classes, creating my lesson plans as I did throughout my teaching career. As I saw some of my fellow yoga teachers struggling with the structure of a class or finding the time to create their own class ideas, I realized that my written plans might make their lives easier as well. And that's what yoga is all about.

Your Yoga Experience: 52 Comprehensive Lessons for Lifelong Practice is a practical guide to the physical, mental, and spiritual practice of yoga. In each of the 52 lessons in this book, a **Focus** topic or aspect of yoga philosophy is introduced and discussed, highlighted by an appropriate quote, then followed by **On the Mat,** where it is applied to the physical (asana) practice on the mat for that day. That asana sequence follows, often using a bracket to indicate a sequence of poses to be done together on each side, with another quote accompanying the final (*Savasana*) pose, and a suggestion for how the focus concept may be applied **Off the Mat,** out in the world and in one's life, which is what yoga is all about.

At the top of each lesson in the book is the symbol of Om ॐ, which is of primary importance in Yoga. The sage Patanjali, in his *Yoga Sutras* written some 2,500 years ago, defines Om as being the name and primordial sound form of the Divine or Consciousness, which when repeated, connects you to your true, inner Self. In the three syllables of the word, pronounced A-U-M, the "A" starts at the back of the throat, comes to the middle of the mouth with the "U", and finishes with the closing of the lips for the "M", creating a humming vibration. Thus, all sounds are made from the word and contained within it. Sogyal Rinpoche writes that the mantra of Om "…is the essence of sound and the embodiment of the truth in the form of sound. Each syllable is impregnated with spiritual power, condenses a spiritual truth, and vibrates with the blessing of the speech of the buddhas."

This book can be used and enjoyed by a wide variety of people at many different levels of experience with yoga. The asana sequences will be invaluable to new teachers who are not yet sure how to prepare their own lessons; to experienced teachers of yoga, who may not have the time to invest in preparing their own lessons; to 'lay' practitioners with experience in doing the poses safely, who would appreciate the structure of prepared lessons; and to less-experienced practitioners who want a written guidebook, while practicing *under the direction of a certified teacher to insure safety.* Yoga and all forms of physical exertion should be preceded by a doctor's examination and permission. There is a photo glossary of the asanas, for the convenience of the reader, listed alphabetically by the English name of each pose. The sequences can be followed as they are written, or embellished with the variations of the poses if known by the practitioner. The amount of poses suggested, along with the focus area, are designed for a class of approximately 80–90 minutes, but of course will vary depending upon the amount of discussion produced and encouraged by each facilitator. The time allotment will no doubt dictate whether poses are omitted or others added. The philosophy and its application alone can be enjoyed by those who find inspiration in the wise individuals quoted in this book, and anyone who is seeking stillness and peace of mind, which can be attained by applying these principles of yoga to daily life.

Blank journal pages are also included in this book and are considered integral to *Svadyaya,* or self-study. As you read the concepts and quotations that are presented here, and reflect upon them in terms of your own attitudes, behaviors, and inner sense of knowing, you are encouraged to write down your thoughts, insights, questions, and ideas. You'll learn so much about yourself if you allow your conscious and subconscious thoughts to come out through your fingers and onto the page, without judgment or censure.

Read, absorb, and savor the mental and spiritual richness and truth of the message of yoga, bask in the physical benefits of the poses, and observe the internal and external transformation that naturally occurs in your life as a result. And as my teacher, Yogi E always says, "Don't believe a thing I'm saying! Experience it for yourself!" Then pass it on…because that is what yoga is all about.

Many Thanks...

My gratitude is boundless for the yoga in my life, which has been instilled, cultivated, enriched, and encouraged by so many people.

I am grateful for and to my husband, Mark, who has been my most ardent cheerleader, supporting and encouraging me in my training and studies, my teaching and writing, always happy to do what he can to create peace and joy in my life. He is always there with a smile to listen to my ideas and my whims, and asks what he can do to "make all my dreams come true." One in a million. I am grateful for and to my children, Eytan Zias and Shira and Rod Lowe, for their love and encouragement and for taking me so seriously, although I'm sure eyes have rolled up as heads have shaken in amusement at times! The amazing, antique Tibetan Prayer Wheel that they gave me upon completion of my training will always be appreciated and treasured.

My late brother, David Allen Chez, tried for so many years to connect me to my spiritual energy, and though I wish we could have shared that while he was alive, I know that all things happen when they happen, and it can't be otherwise. I believe that David started me on my path and is integrally responsible somehow for my spiritual epiphany and growth, and for that I am deeply grateful.

I am forever grateful to my teacher and trainer, Eric Walrabenstein (Yogi E), who introduced the beauty and richness of yoga to me and its daily application for fulfillment and peace in every moment of every day. I thank Eric and my many other teachers for imparting their knowledge, love, and light with the sincere desire to share what has benefited and enriched their own lives, displaying 'mudita', a joy in the joy of others. I thank my fellow yoga practitioners and my yoga students for all that I have learned from them, for the ways that I have benefited from their presence, their questions, and their input.

I humbly thank my many friends and relatives who have been supportive and encouraging both of my journey and this book, ready to lend an ear, offer constructive criticism, a pat on the back, or words of advice when needed. My love and thanks to Nomi Sharron, who graciously allowed me to include her poem *Consciousness* in my book, thereby infusing it with her spirit.

This book could not have been accomplished without the specific contributions of the many people who have shared in the making of my vision. Thanks to Melissa Hawkins, for her positive energy and inspiration as the model for the cover and pose glossary of this book. Thanks to Carol Berger Taylor, the artist, metalworker, and photographer, who painstakingly and beautifully photographed Melissa. Thanks to my teacher, Laura Kessler, who edited the sequences in this book and added to the safety and enjoyment of the practitioners who will follow them in each lesson. Thanks to Amber Mellano for her technical finesse and support, and her patience with me for my lack of it. Thanks to Helene Sabel for her time and her sharp skills in proofreading this manuscript. None of this would have been possible without the professionalism, talent, support, and good nature of Michele, Ronda, and Diane at 1106 Design. Many thanks.

Namaste,

Sandi

Consciousness

by
Nomi Sharron (Portugal, 2006)

Consciousness is the key and the doorway
    The opening and the stepping through
    The path and the walking
It is our North Star illuminating our way
    The North Star
    Illumination
       The Way

Consciousness is the Pillar of Fire that guides
    Our desert wanderings
       And the peace of Promised Land
It is memories before time birthed in light
    Transcendent worlds resonant
       Beyond
       And beyond
          And deep within

Consciousness is the seed and the blossoming
    The fruit and the fruition
    Sylvan smiles of early morning dew
It is the mountain and the climbing
       The dancer evolving into dance
       Footsteps preceding feet
       The toucher and the touching
          And the touch

Consciousness is the breeze of small wings flapping
    Songs and silence of the sky
    Soul journeys guided through infinity
        By landmarks of love
It is Truth on the ragged tongue of the wind
    Earth damp solitude
    Falling into
        One-ness
        Divinity
            Transformation

Consciousness is curiosity opening a flower
    Caress of children's wonderment
    Colours of infinity
    Clouds raining
        Affirmation
It is orbit of devotion unbounded
    Gravity suspended
    Knowledge held in stones
        The heart of the universe
        Beating
            In each breast

Consciousness is the end of separation
    Expansion of the unity of all
    Rolling back space through
        Evolutions of eternity
        Breaking through the skin
            Of time
It is weightlessness of moments uncoiling
    No end no beginning
    Fullness of circle
        Gratitude spilling
        From the womb of
            The world

Consciousness is hard rocks of humility
 Night sighs threaded through water
 Storms and their abatement
  Unfolding grace
It is a weave of angels whispering
 Karma decoded
 Celebration of
  Innocence
  And knowing
   And not knowing

Consciousness is meeting with Mystery
 Meaning magnified in
 Unspoken stories
 Spirals of spirits
 Heralding Heaven
  Hereafter
  Here
It is the whitened bones of the world laid bare
 Taste of newborn laughter
 Warm mantle of stars
 Eyes of moon magic
  Weeping love

Consciousness is timeless wakeful dreaming
 Waterfalls of yearning
 Unnameable oracles
 Breath of Being held
  On butterfly wings
It is the rhythms of Mother Earth birthing
 Movement and stillness
 Wisdom rooted by trees
  Sacred surrender

Consciousness is a web of prayer
    Mapping miracles
    Drawing close horizons of
        The farthest shore
Consciousness is the sleeping world
    And our awakening

Consciousness is the Source
    Our essence
        And our journeying
            And our homecoming

Consciousness is

Table of Contents

Patanjali's Ashtanga Yoga (Eight Limbs)
From *Patanjali's Yoga Sutras*

Yamas: *Ethical Disciplines* (Relationship to Others)
- Ahimsa: Non-harming
- Satya: Truth
- Asteya: Non-stealing
- Brahmacharya: Moving toward the Divine
- Aparigraha: Non-hoarding, Non-attachment

Niyamas: *Personal Disciplines* (Relationship to Self)
- Saucha: Purity
- Santosha: Contentment
- Tapas: Discipline
- Svadhyaya: Self-study
- Ishvara Pranidhana: Surrender

Asana: Physical Postures

Pranayama: Breath and Energy Control

Pratyahara: Sensory Withdrawal

Dharana: Concentration

Dhyana: Meditation

Samadhi: Oneness, Absorption

Lesson One

Focus: *Ahimsa* — Non-harming and *Satya* — Truth

Ahimsa means the non-harming of all sentient beings, including ourselves, by our thoughts, words, and actions. This concept brings an awareness of the importance of performing kind deeds, sharing kind words, and trying to see the best in people and situations. *Ahimsa* encourages a gentleness with ourselves and others, which includes not being judgmental or critical.

Satya is being truthful and honest, though discrimination is urged so that we are not harming others or ourselves by speaking a painful truth that may not need to be said.

> *"Hear from the heart wordless mysteries!*
> *Understand what cannot be understood...*
> *In our stone-dark hearts there burns a fire*
> *That burns all veils to their root and foundation.*
> *When the veils are burned away,*
> *The heart will understand completely...*
> *Ancient love will unfold ever-fresh forms*
> *In the heart of the Spirit, in the core of the heart."*
> ~ Rumi

On the Mat: Open and breathe into the heart space, that deep place within where we feel trust and love, self-confidence, and the truth of who we are. Listen to your body for clues as to how far to go within a pose without causing yourself harm.

Awakening the Body: Opening the heart space

- **Reclining Bound Angle Pose** (Supta Baddha Konasana)
  Blanket
- **Cat-Cow** (Marjaryasana), **Twist**
- **Downward-Facing Dog** (Adho Mukha Svanasana)
- **Sun Salutation** (Surya Namaskar)
  - **Runner's Lunge**
  - **Low Lunge** (Anjaneyasana)
- **Standing Forward Bend** (Uttanasana)

Standing
- **Warrior II** (Virabhadrasana II)
- **Reverse Warrior**
- **Side-Angle Pose** (Parsvakonasana)
- **Yoga Mudra** *Strap*

Mat
- **Child's Pose** (Balasana)
- **Thunderbolt Pose** (Vajrasana)
- **Seated Bound Angle Pose** (Baddha Konasana)
- **Seated Forward Bend** (Paschimotanasana)
- **Thread the Needle**
- **Half Lord of the Fishes** (Ardha Matsyendrasana)
- **Knees to Chest** (Apanasana)
- **Happy Baby Pose** (Ananda Balasana)
- **Corpse Pose** (Savasana)

"When the veils are burned away,
the heart will understand completely..."

Off the Mat: Throughout your day, take the time to listen to your heart, trust your intuition, and heed your truth. Perform a kindness for yourself or others during the day. How does this make you feel?

Focus: *Asteya* — Non-stealing

Asteya refers not just to the stealing of material objects, but also of others' time when we make them wait, their ideas if we present them as our own, or their attention if we draw it away and towards ourselves. *Asteya* means not depriving others of what is rightfully theirs or not taking something that has not been given freely. By stealing we are acting out our dissatisfaction with our present reality and showing our discontent with ourselves for who and what we are.

Stealing then leads to breaking other principles as well, like *Ahimsa* (Non-harming of others), *Satya* (Truthfulness), and *Aparigraha* (Non-attachment to greed or desire).

> *"We are enough as we are...All deficiencies*
> *are perceived deficiencies."*
> ~ Yogi Amrit Desai

On the Mat: Don't steal from yourself by not breathing fully, by going past your edge or not far enough in a pose, or by not giving yourself due credit for your efforts.

Awakening the Body: Connecting movement with breath
- **Easy Seat** (Sukhasana), with **Three-Part Breathing**
- **Cat-Cow** (Marjaryasana)
- **Child's Pose** (Balasana)
- **Downward Facing Dog** (Adho Mukha Svanasana)
- **Standing Forward Fold** (Uttanasana)

Standing
- **Standing Stretches**
- **Sun Salutation** (Surya Namaskar)
  - **Runner's Lunge**
  - **Plank Pose**
  - **Side Plank Pose** (Vasisthasana)
- **Mountain Pose** (Tedasana)
- **Triangle Pose** (Trikonasana) *Block*
- **Wide-legged Forward Fold** (Prasarita Padottanasana), Twist
- **Cow Face Pose** (Gamukhasana) *Strap*
- **Yoga Mudra**
- **Standing Forward Fold** (Uttanasana)

Mat
- **Child's Pose** (Balasana)
- **Head to Knee Pose** (Janu Sirsasana)
- **Wide-Angle Seated Forward Fold** (Upavistha Konasana)
- **Supine Twists**
- **Corpse Pose** (Savasana)

"Who is rich? He who is satisfied with his lot."
~ The Talmud, Pirkei Avot

Off the Mat: Bring your attention and awareness to all that you already have to be grateful for, rather than what you feel you lack. When you feel fulfilled with what you have and who you are, you will find you have much to offer others in time, energy, and love. What will you give, rather than take, today?

Lesson Three

Focus: *Brahmacharya* — Moderation in All Things

Brahmacharya has been interpreted as a Pathway to the Divine, Walking with a Higher Power, or Living in Higher Awareness. In most texts this has been taken further to mean the retaining of one's sexual energy through celibacy in order to experience that awareness to the fullest. I prefer to understand it as Nischala Joy Devi expresses it, as a concept of moderation and balance, through which "...*we are able to orchestrate the glorious dance between our Divine nature and human nature.*"

> *"Devoted to living a balanced and moderate life, the scope of one's life force becomes boundless."*
> ~ *Yoga Sutras*, II:38

On the Mat: Notice your tendency to leave the place of moderation and go to extremes, either by working over your edge in a pose or not working hard enough. Connect to breath and enjoy the feeling of calm while in balance.

Awakening the Body: Finding a place of balance
- On back, **Supine Twists**
- **Reclined Big Toe Pose** (Supta Padangusthasana) *Strap*
- **Legs Up the Wall** (Viparita Karani), on *Block*
- **Table Top**
- **Child's Pose** (Balasana)
- **Standing Forward Fold** (Uttanasana)

Standing
- **Mountain Pose** (Tedasana)
- **Warrior I** (Virabhadrasana I)
- **Intense Side Stretch Pose** (Parsvottanasana) *Blocks*
- **Warrior III** (Virabhadrasana III) *Block*
- **Tree Pose** (Vrksasana)
- **Half Sun Salutation** (Ardha Surya Namaskar)
- **Standing Forward Fold** (Uttanasana)

Mat
- **Garland Pose** (Malasana)
- **Noose Pose** (Pasasana) *Blanket* under feet
- **Boat Pose** (Navasana)
- **Marichi's Twist** (Marichyasana)
- **Supine Twists**
- **Corpse Pose** (Savasana)

"Yoga is not for one who eats too much, or for one who fasts too much, nor sleeps too much or sleeps too little, but instead lives in a harmonious flow along the middle path."
~ Bhagavad Gita

Off the Mat: Notice how you feel when you leave the place of balance and go to a place of extremes: Eating or sleeping too little or too much, working, exercising, or engaging in one specific activity too much. Does this deplete your energy? How does this serve you?

𝕱ocus: *Aparigraha* — Non-attachment

If we are attached to the belief that our happiness always depends on something outside of ourselves — for example, material objects, relationships, status, level of performance, etc. — we will constantly be seeking to own more and/or be other than we are, and never be content with the way things are at the moment. While we continue to work toward our goals, we can enjoy the happiness that arises by dealing with what is at the moment, rather than how we think it should be.

In addition, being attached to the results of our actions, over which we have no control, causes disappointment and unhappiness. By acting from our truth and a sincere motivation to give something or help someone with 'no strings attached,' thereby letting go of the need for the response that we had anticipated, we can avoid the dis-ease and continue having peace of mind.

"We have the right to action, but not to the results of our action."
~ Bhagavad Gita

O𝕟 𝕥𝕙𝕖 𝕸at: Let go of something in your practice today that you feel attached to, perhaps *Ego:* Having to do the poses as well or better than others, rather than letting go and accepting however you are showing up on your mat; or *Security:* Having to perform the same poses in the same way, rather than letting go and try-ing new poses, without preconditions for how you will do them.

Awakening the Body: Letting go of the results
- **Easy Seat** (Sukhasana), with Sama-Vritti (Even) Breathing
- **Cat-Cow** (Marjaryasana)
  - Twist
  - Alternate arm/leg
- **Child's Pose** (Balasana)
- **Extended Puppy Pose** (Uttana Shishosana)
- **Child's Pose** (Balasana)
- **Downward Facing Dog** (Adho Mukha Svanasana)
- **Standing Forward Fold** (Uttanasana)

Standing
- **Half Sun Salutation** (Ardha Surya Namaskar)
- **Warrior II** (Virabhadrasana II)
- **Reverse Warrior**
- **Side Angle Pose** (Parsvakonasana)
- **Eagle Pose** (Garudasana) *Strap*
- **Yoga Mudra**
- **Standing Forward Fold** (Uttanasana)

Mat
- **Child's Pose** (Balasana)
- **Bound Angle** (Baddha Konasana), fold
- **Half Lord of the Fishes** (Ardha Matsyendrasana)
- **Supine Twists**
- **Corpse Pose** (Savasana)

"Our thoughts are ours, their ends none of our own."
~ Shakespeare, Hamlet

Off the Mat: During the day, notice if you have an expectation of a specific result of your actions. Be aware of how you feel when you let go of the expectation, and just deal with what is instead of what you think should be. Practice taking a deep breath, smiling and going on with your day.

Focus: *Saucha* — Purity and Cleanliness

Everything in your life has an effect upon you: what you eat, hear, see, think, the people with whom you socialize. A clear indication of this is to be aware of how you feel after eating certain foods, listening to certain music, watching specific television programs or being in a person's company.

One effective yardstick is to ask yourself: *How is this serving me? Is this disturbing my peace and stillness or increasing my sense of well-being and happiness?* See your choices in terms of nourishment vs. toxicity for your body, your mind, and your spirit.

> *"If you realized the destructive impact of self-defeating thoughts and toxic emotions, you would immediately let them go."*
> ~ Yogi Amrit Desai

On the Mat: Cleanse your mind of toxic thoughts by feeling the effects of each pose, rather than attaching labels or judgments to your performance. The body will physically be cleansed of toxins through twists.

Awakening the Body: Just feel
- **Easy Seat** (Sukhasana), with **Ujjai Breathing**
- **Extended Puppy Pose** (Uttana Shishosana)
- **Thunderbolt Pose** (Vajrasana)
  - Twists
  - Side Stretches
- **Cat-Cow** (Marjaryasana)
- **Downward Facing Dog** (Adho Mukha Svanasana)
- **Child's Pose** (Balasana)
- **Dolphin Pose**
- **Standing Forward Fold** (Uttanasana)
  - Twist

Standing
- **Chair Pose** (Uttkatasana), Twist
- **Triangle Pose** (Trikonasana) *Block*
- **Wide-legged Forward Fold** (Prasarita Padottanasana)
  - Twist
- **Yoga Mudra**

Mat
- **Bound Angle Pose** (Baddha Konasana)
  - **Forward Fold**
  - Twist
- **Seated Forward Fold** (Paschimottanasana)
- **Half Lord of Fishes Pose** (Ardha Matsyendrasana)
- **Supine Twists**
- **Corpse Pose** (Savasana)

"…Our intention is to heal our body, clear our mind, and purify our heart, and bring them into alignment with our highest potential."
~ Yogi Amrit Desai

Off the Mat: Whether choosing foods, music, entertainment, or friends, ask yourself: "How does this serve my stillness and well-being?" Listen, then trust the truth of your answer.

Lesson Six

𝓕**ocus:** *Santosha* — Unconditional Contentment

If we do only what we like and depend upon outside objects and activities to keep us happy, then our happiness is limited and conditional, however, we know that life isn't always what we want. Therefore, if we can find a way of finding peace and contentment in any situation, whether it's a challenging yoga pose or a frustrating traffic jam, then unconditional happiness is always available. That is *Santosha*.

"When at peace and content with oneself and
others, supreme joy is celebrated."

~ Nischala Joy Devi

On the Mat: You can find your place of peace and calm within you by connecting with breath, regardless of the pose. Can you rest with what is arising, rather than criticizing yourself and trying to change it? The reality of the pose is not the obstacle, how you relate to your perceived limitations in it can be.

Awakening the Body: Connect to breath

Standing (Notice your reaction to this change in sequence.)
- **Side Stretches**
- **Sun Salutation** (Surya Namaskar)
  - **Runner's Lunge**
  - **Low Lunge** (Anjaneyasana)
  - **Downward Facing Dog** (Adho Mukha Svanasana)
- **Warrior II** (Virabhadrasana II) ⎫
- **Reverse Warrior** ⎬
- **Side Angle Pose** (Parsvakonasana) ⎭
- **Tree Pose** (Vrksasana)
- **Standing Forward Fold** (Uttanasana)

Mat
- **Child's Pose** (Balasana)
- **Plank Pose**
- **Pigeon Pose** (Eka Pada Rajakapotasana) *Blanket*
- **Downward Facing Dog** (Adho Mukha Svanasana)
- **Child's Pose** (Balasana)
- **Easy Seat** (Sukhasana)
  - Fold
  - Twist
- **Supine Twists**
- **Corpse Pose** (Savasana)

"By contentment, supreme joy is gained."
~ Patanjali, *Yoga Sutras* II:2

Off the Mat: Return to focus on your breath when situations around you threaten to disturb your inner peace. Deeply inhaling and slowly exhaling calms you and gives you time to respond, rather than react. Set an intention to stay poised and calm regardless of what may arise around you.

Lesson Seven

ℱocus: *Tapas* — Internal Fire, Discipline, and Commitment

Determination and intensity to stick to a diet, to finish that term paper, or to practice yoga and meditate daily is the burning and purification of *Tapas*. *Tapas* is practiced not in order to achieve a goal, per se, but rather it is following the passion and doing the work to make our intentions a reality. Personal transformation occurs by noticing the effect of this discipline on our own experience.

> *"Tapas as a practice is not about what you get, …it is about what you give. Whether you are driven or resistant, the medicine is the same: do what is truly possible with unwavering commitment to giving yourself to the moment. Without this intention, practice becomes just another task to be completed and it loses its ability to transform."*
>
> ~ Judith Lasater

On the Mat: Setting the intention to be on this mat right now and implementing the discipline to follow through until the end of the session will yield the reward of discovering your inner strength, your internal fire.

Awakening the Body: Give yourself to the moment
- **Thunderbolt Pose** (Vajrasana), Fold, Side Stretches *Block*
- **Gate Pose** (Parighasana) *Block*
- **Cat-Cow** (Marjaryasana)
- **Downward Facing Dog** (Adho Mukha Svanasana)
- **Standing Forward Fold** (Uttanasana)

Standing
- **Upward Salute** (Urdhva Hastasana)
- **Sun Salutation** (Surya Namaskar)
  - **Runner's Lunge**
  - **Plank Pose**
  - **Side Plank Pose** (Vasistasana)
  - **Downward Facing Dog** (Adho Mukha Svanasana)
- **Standing Forward Fold** (Uttanasana)
- **Mountain Pose** (Tedasana)
- **Chair Pose** (Uttkatasana)
- **Half Sun Salutation**

Mat
- **Seated Forward Fold** (Paschimottanasa)
- **Marichi's Twist** (Marichyasana)
- **Supine Twists**
- **Corpse Pose** (Savasana)

"Without Tapas your journey is chaotic, directionless and without structure. Tapas is the very essence of the journey. It adds richness and meaning to the path. …The most enlightened Yogi and the most successful entrepreneur have something in common: both are infused with the spirit of Tapas."
~ "Tapas: Tempering the Fire Within"

Off the Mat: Apply this commitment and intensity to accomplishing even one thing that you have been putting off, by setting an intention to give yourself fully to the moment. Ask yourself how this served you, then go on to the next thing, then the next.

Lesson Eight

Focus: *Svadyaya* — Self-study, Introspection, Self-observation

Whether we practice self-study through journaling or meditation, mindfulness practice is of the utmost importance. Only by knowing ourselves can we understand our perceptions of our experiences, and only by sitting in quiet can we know if something rings true for us. As we observe ourselves with detachment and lack of judgment through yoga, on and off the mat, we can develop a sense of awareness to assess what our needs truly are. *Svadyaya* is going inside of ourselves and finding out what and why.

"Often we tell ourselves, 'Don't just sit there, do something!'
But when we practice awareness, we discover…that the opposite
may be more helpful: 'Don't just do something, sit there!'
We must learn to stop from time to time in order to see clearly."
~ Thich Nhat Hanh

On the Mat: Notice your reaction to the challenges you find in certain poses, whether it's frustration and impatience, or praise and arrogance. Go inside and find the what and why.

Awakening the Body: Into feeling, out of thought
- **Child's Pose** (Balasana)
- **Cat-Cow** (Marjaryasana)
  - Twist
  - Alternate arm/leg
- **Downward Facing Dog** (Adho Mukha Svanasana)
- **Low Lunges** (Anjaneyasana)
- **Child's Pose** (Balasana)
- **Downward Facing Dog** (Adho Mukha Svanasana)
- **Standing Forward Fold** (Uttanasana)

Standing
- **Sun Salutation** (Surya Namaskar)
  - **Plank Pose**
  - **Cobra** (Bhujangasana)
  - **Downward Facing Dog** (Adho Mukha Svanasana)
- **Standing Forward Fold** (Uttanasana) ⎫
- **Triangle Pose** (Trikonasana) ⎬
- **Reverse Triangle** ⎭
- **Yoga Mudra**

Mat
- **Thread the Needle**
- **Child's Pose** (Balasana)
- **Head to Knee Pose** (Janu Sirsasana), Twist
- **Bound Angle Pose** (Baddha Konasana)
- **Figure Four Stretch**
- **Supine Twists**
- **Corpse Pose** (Savasana)

"The basic condition for being happy is our consciousness of being happy...When we have a toothache, we know that not having a toothache is a wonderful thing. But when we do not have a toothache, we are still not happy. A non-toothache is very pleasant."
~ Thich Nhat Hanh

Off the Mat: Make a mental note of your reactions to your daily experiences and how they compare to those in your poses. Can you go to the place of feeling while you're sitting in traffic as though it were another balancing pose on the mat?

Focus: *Ishvara Pranidhana* — Surrender to the Divine

'Surrender' is often a concept that triggers many emotions, but in yoga this is not a word of weakness and passivity, but rather an active act of letting go, a fortifying challenge to reach inside and bring the best part of ourselves to the surface. The 'Divine' is also often a controversial idea, but here again we can define this as anything from our own higher nature to our personal perception of trusting in something greater than ourselves.

Many of us have a need for controlling situations and others to the detriment of our peace of mind and stillness when that control eludes us. When we can surrender that control, we begin to have a relationship with our inner guidance and feel trust that we are part of a larger consciousness. Our perspective changes from the obsession with "I", to the awareness of "I am", reuniting us with our true Self and bringing us back to inner peace and balance.

> *"Through surrender the aspirant's ego is effaced, and…
> grace…pours down upon him like a torrential rain."*
> ~ B.K.S. Iyengar

On the Mat: Notice how your mind and body respond during your practice when you let go of tension, gripping, or impatience, and when you surrender to something outside of yourself while being fully in the moment.

Awakening the Body: Just... let... go

- **Reclined Bound Angle** (Supta Baddha Konasana) *Blanket, Blocks*
- **Legs Up the Wall** (Viparita Karani), on *Block*
- **Happy Baby** (Ananda Balasana)
- **Child's Pose** (Balasana)
- **Extended Puppy Pose** (Uttana Shishosana)
- **Downward Facing Dog** (Adho Mukha Svanasana)
- **Standing Forward Fold** (Uttanasana)

Standing

- **Mountain Pose** (Tedasana)
- **Tree Pose** (Vrksasana)
- **Eagle Pose** (Garudasana)
- **Yoga Mudra**
- **Chair Pose** (Uttkatasana), Twist
- **Half Sun Salutation** (Ardha Surya Namaskar)
- **Standing Forward Fold** (Uttanasana)
  - **Big Toe Pose** (Padangusthasana)

Mat

- **Cat-Cow** (Marjaryasana)
- **Seated Forward Fold** (Paschimottanasana)
- **Half Lord of the Fishes** (Ardha Matsyendrasana)
- **Supine Twists**
- **Corpse Pose** (Savasana)

"Let go or get dragged."
~ Lama Surya Das

Off the Mat: Whenever you encounter tension or frustration during your day, connect to breath and surrender needing control of the situation. Notice how it serves you to mindfully respond, rather than automatically react, and see how that affects others around you.

*F*ocus: *Asana* — The Physical Postures

The third limb of yoga, the physical form of the postures, is a metaphor for all other experiences (forms) in life. The mat is a place to practice yoga, that is, a place to have your buttons pushed, your habits revealed, and then see how you react in order to learn to be with what is out in the world and find happiness in each moment.

It is through awareness of what does or does not serve you that any transformation in your life will occur, not through any forced change of behavior. We learn to observe ourselves without judgments and criticisms, and be OK with what is.

> *"It's not important how you are,*
> *but how you are with how you are."*
> ~ Eric Walrabenstein (Yogi E)

On the Mat: The Yoga mat is a laboratory, a place to reveal who and where you are inside. Be mindful and aware of your reactions to the poses, without making judgments of your performance, then return to feeling and to the breath.

Awakening the Body: Deal with what is arising in the moment

- **Easy Seat** (Sukhasana), Stretches
- **Reclining Big Toe Pose** (Supta Padangusthasana) *Strap*
- **Child's Pose** (Balasana)
- **Cat-Cow** (Marjaryasana)
- **Side Plank Pose** (Vasisthasana)
- **Downward Facing Dog** (Adho Mukha Svanasana)
- **Runner's Lunge**
- **Downward Facing Dog** (Adho Mukha Svanasana)
- **Standing Forward Fold** (Uttanasana)

Standing

- **Upward Salute** (Urdhva Hastasana)
- **Warrior II** (Virabhadrasana II)
- **Reverse Warrior**
- **Side Angle Pose** (Parsvokonasana)
- **Wide-legged Forward Fold** (Prasarita Padottanasana)
- **Mountain Pose** (Tedasana)
- **Yoga Mudra**

Mat

- **Bridge Pose** (Setu Bandha Sarvangasana)
- **Knees to Chest** (Apanasana)
- **Reclining Bound Angle** (Supta Baddha Konasana)
- **Supine Twists**
- **Corpse Pose** (Savasana)

"Every time you judge yourself, you break your own heart..."
~ Swami Kripalvananda

Off the Mat: Apply the insights you have gleaned about yourself from your mat practice today and see how they correspond to your reactions to your life experiences off the mat.

Focus: *Pranayama* — Breath and Energy Control

Prana is the innate energetic intelligence that animates all of life. By removing impediments to its free flow, *Prana* is able to spontaneously bring the body/mind into its natural balance and rhythm, restoring optimum health and ease.

There are many *Pranayama* techniques, but the three-part breathing is basic to both meditation and asana practices. This involves a deep inhalation through the nostrils, filling up first the abdomen, the diaphragm, then the heart space with air like a balloon. The exhalation is in the reverse order.

> *"Asana is meditation on the body, Pranayama is meditation on the breath and subtle energy currents within us, and then we work with the mind directly, with the ultimate aim of transcending body and mind and experiencing the higher Self."*
> ~ Swami Karunanand

On the Mat: Practicing mindfulness and awareness, notice where your breath naturally originates in each of the poses. Then return to connect to your three-part breathing practice.

Awakening the Body: *"Wherever the mind goes, the Prana follows."*
(St. Thirumular)

- **Easy Seat** (Sukhasana), with Three-Part Breathing
- **Cow Face** Arms (Gomukhasana) *Strap*
- **Gate Pose** (Parighasana) *Block*
- **Child's Pose** (Balasana)
- **Downward Facing Dog** (Adho Mukha Svanasana)
- **Standing Forward Fold** (Uttanasana)

Standing

- **Chair Pose** (Uttkatasana), Twist
- **Sun Salutation** (Surya Namaskar)
  - **Runner's Lunge**
  - **Low Lunge** (Anjaneyasana), Twist
- **Warrior I** (Virabhadrasana I) ⎫
- **Crescent Pose** ⎬
- **Mountain Pose** (Tedasana) ⎭
- **Eagle Pose** (Garudasana)
- **Yoga Mudra**

Mat

- **Bound Angle Pose** (Bhaddha Konasana)
  - Fold
  - Twist
- **Upward Plank Pose** (Purvottanasana)
- **Seated Forward Fold** (Paschimottanasana)
- **Supine Twists**
- **Corpse Pose** (Savasana)

*"When the breath is steady or unsteady, so is the mind, and
with it the yogi. Hence, the breath should be controlled."*
~ Hatha Yoga Pradipika, Ch. II.2

Off the Mat: During your daily activities, notice where your
breath originates. Return to your three-part breathing and be aware
of any changes in your mind, body, and energy. You are in control.

Lesson Twelve

𝒥ocus: *Pratyahara* — Withdrawal of the Senses

Notice how Patanjali's Yoga Sutras go from the gross to the subtle. We first must deal with our principles *(Yamas)* and behaviors *(Niyamas)*, then the physical *(Asana)* and breathing practices *(Pranayama)*, and now we are readying ourselves for the last several limbs, the most subtle forms of the mind.

Pratyahara is about being able to remain in the middle of a stimulating environment and consciously not reacting to it, however, there is a difference between withdrawal and escape. When you escape an unwanted situation by using outside, stimulating experiences, you are taken further from yourself by interfering with your intention of being present to what is happening. Withdrawing the senses from an outside stimulus, however, keeps you "in the world, but not of it."

> *"The senses are like a mirror. Turned outward, they reflect the outside; turned inward, they reflect the pure light [and] find peace by taking the form of the mind itself."*
> ~ Sri Swami Satchidananda

On the Mat: Notice how you are reacting to any discomfort or to your performance in a pose. Bring yourself to a place of feeling rather than thought. You can choose to withdraw your energy from your thoughts about the pose and focus instead on the pose itself.

Awakening the Body: Just this

- **Thunderbolt Pose** (Vajrasana), Stretches *Block, Strap*
- **Child's Pose** (Balasana)
- **Downward Facing Dog** (Adho Mukha Svanasana)
- **Plank Pose**
- **Cobra** (Bhujangasana)
- **Child's Pose** (Balasana)
- **Downward Facing Dog** (Adho Mukha Svanasana)
- **Standing Forward Fold** (Uttanasana)

Standing

- **Upward Salute** (Urdhva Hastasana)
- **Tree Pose** (Vrksasana)
- **Yoga Mudra**
- **Triangle Pose** (Trikonasana) ⎫
- **Intense Side Stretch** (Parsvottanasana) *Blocks* ⎬
- **Half Sun Salutation** (Ardha Surya Namaskar)

Mat

- **Boat Pose** (Navasana)
- **Bridge Pose** (Setu Bandha Sarvangasana)
- **Figure Four Stretch**
- **Supine Twists**
- **Corpse Pose** (Savasana)

Notice the practice of *Pratyahara* in your Savasana: First stage is physiological relaxation...muscles, breath, letting go of tension. The second stage affects the mental level, where there is a sense that one is withdrawing from the external world without losing contact with it. There are sounds, but they do not create a disturbance in the body or mind. This is the experience of *Pratyahara*, this state of non-reaction to any stimuli around you.

Off the Mat: Notice your habit of wanting to escape a difficulty you may meet in your day and how you may try to accomplish that. Then ask yourself how it would serve you if you were to face it and perhaps withdraw into breath for centering.

Lesson Thirteen

Focus: *Dharana* — Concentration, Exclusive One-Pointedness

When we sit in concentration, we are focusing on one thing, while excluding all others. This one-pointed focus could be on a mantra or single sound, on the breath, on a specific object in our awareness, or whatever clears our mind of all the extraneous thoughts that cloud our thinking and prevent us from being in the present moment.

Have you noticed that when you're reading a riveting book, absorbed in a compelling movie, or involved in an interesting discussion, time seems to fly without your awareness of the fleeting moments? This is concentration even without the intention to focus.

> *"Yoga is the stilling of the fluctuations of the mind.*
> *Then the Seer abides in her own true nature."*
> ~ Patanjali, *Yoga Sutras,* II:2

On the Mat: The invitation is to focus on a specific body part while you are in a pose at the exclusion of all other stimuli. Notice how long you can concentrate on one thing before the mind is already fluttering to another.

Awakening the Body: Focus on *

- **Easy Seat** (Sukhasana), Stretches *Strap* (*shoulder blades)
- **Child's Pose** (Balasana)
- **Downward Facing Dog** (Adho Mukha Svanasana) (*thumb mounds)
  - **Three-legged Dog**
  - **Fire Hydrant Pose**
- **Child's Pose** (Balasana)
- **Side Plank Pose** (Vasisthansana) (*shoulder)
- **Downward Facing Dog** (Adho Mukha Svanasana)
- **Standing Forward Fold** (Uttanasana)

Standing

- **Chair Pose** (Uttkatasana) *Block* (*tailbone)
- **Warrior II** (Virabhadrasana II) ⎱
- **Reverse Warrior** (*breath) ⎰
- **Side Angle Pose** (Parsvokonasana) ⎰
- **Standing Forward Fold**, (Uttanasana) Twist

Mat

- **Child's Pose** (Balasana)
- **Thunderbolt Pose** (Vajrasana), Stretches
- **Head to Knee Pose** (Janu Sirsasana), Twist (*flexed foot)
- **Supine Twists**
- **Corpse Pose** (Savasana)

*"Only in quiet waters do things mirror themselves undistorted.
Only in a quiet mind is adequate perception of the world."*
~ Hans Margolius

Off the Mat: Try to set aside a quiet time each day. Close your eyes, and concentrate on one sound, word, or object. Expect the mind to chatter because that's what it does, but just say "not now," and bring your attention back to your focus as many times as it takes.

Focus: *Dhyana* — Meditation, Inclusive One-flowingness
Samadhi — Absorption, Integration

While sitting in meditation, practicing the technique of 'Bare Attention' allows you to be aware of everything all around you non-selectively. It is an un-focusing, an inclusion of all sensations and objects in your awareness into the whole picture, including your thoughts, all holding the same weight and importance.

Without staring or focusing on one specific object in front of you, soften your eyes and see everything in your vision, top to bottom, side to side. Include what you hear. Include the thoughts that float in and out: Wall, birdsong, thought, emotional feeling, physical sensation, another thought, another sound...All part of the whole, all noted equally. Without giving one item more weight and power than another, we can keep our inner place of peace and balance. This feeling of oneness is approaching *Samadhi.*

> *"The you that goes in one side of the meditation experience is not the same you that comes out the other side."*
> ~ Bhante Henepola Gunaratana

On the Mat: Pay attention to all parts of the body, to all cells in the body, to all feelings in the body, equally. Be in the experience, in the whole picture.

Awakening the Body: Feel every cell equally
- **Extended Puppy Pose** (Uttana Shishasana)
- **Cat-Cow** (Marjaryasana)
- **Downward Facing Dog** (Adho Mukha Svanasana)
- **Standing Forward Fold** (Uttanasana)
  - Twist
  - **Big Toe Pose** (Padangusthasana)

Standing
- **Warrior I** (Virabhadrasana I) ⎫
- **Warrior III** (Virabhadrasana III) ⎭
- **Triangle Pose** (Trikonasana) *Block* ⎫
- **Reverse Triangle** ⎭
- **Yoga Mudra**

Mat
- **Boat Pose** (Navasana)
- **Easy Seat** (Sukhasana), Fold, Twist
- **Bridge Pose** (Setu Bandha Sarvangasana)
- **Supine Twists**
- **Corpse Pose** (Savasana)

"Samadhi is the state in which you are aware on a cellular level of the underlying oneness of the universe…The concept of Samadhi brings with it the possibility of a deep hope about our growth as human beings. Patanjali teaches us that we are always capable of experiencing Samadhi, that at any moment we can become whole and fully present. If we understand this, that understanding becomes a fundamental acknowledgment of our true nature. Paradoxically, it seems that we need the journey—the journey of yoga—to discover what was present inside us all along."
~ Judith Lasater

Off the Mat: During your day, when meeting with an annoying or uncomfortable experience such as traffic or a line at the supermarket, practice Bare Attention as you include all people, sights, sounds, and thoughts into one whole picture, and note if and how this changes your experience.

Focus: *Samskaras* — Mental Impressions or Grooves from the Past

Samskaras are habitual patterns, tendencies, or unconscious conditioning from our past experiences, which act like little ruts in a muddy road. The next time a car travels that road, the tires will want to slip right back into those hardened grooves rather than attempt to avoid them and create new tracks.

Are you stuck in a groove that makes you afraid to try something new or get out of your comfort zone? Perhaps living your day mindfully and on purpose, rather than habitually according to old beliefs, will open you to allowing new tracks to be formed.

"What you are is what you have been.
What you will be is what you do now."
~ The Buddha

On the Mat: Notice your habits while doing the poses. Are you automatically moving into a pose, or are you aware of each moment, mindful of each step of the way? Take care not to allow preconceived beliefs of how you think you should be in each pose to take you out of the experience of how you are.

Awakening the Body: Step by step
- **Thunderbolt Pose** (Vajrasana), Stretches
- **Child's Pose** (Balasana)
- **Cat-Cow** (Marjaryasana)
- **Downward Facing Dog** (Adho Mukha Svanasana) ⎞
- **Runner's Lunge** ⎬
- **Plank Pose** ⎠
- **Standing Forward Fold** (Uttanasana)
  - **Wrist Stand** (Padahastasana)

Standing
- **Mountain Pose** (Tedasana)
- **Warrior II** (Virabhadrasana II) ⎞
- **Reverse Warrior** ⎬
- **Side Angle Pose** (Parsvakonasana) ⎠
- **Wide-legged Forward Fold** (Prasaritta Padottanasana)
- **Standing Forward Fold** (Uttanasana)

Mat
- **Plank Pose**
- **Pigeon Pose** (Eka Pada Rajakapotasana) *Blanket*
- **Downward Facing Dog** (Adho Mukha Svanasana)
- **Cow Face Pose** (Gomukhasana)
- **Seated Forward Fold** (Paschimottanasana)
- **Supine Twists**
- **Corpse Pose** (Savasana)

"Whichever belief system you subscribe to, know that you possess the power to affect your life's patterns and dreams. When a thought, feeling, or situation arises, it will naturally flow into the groove that presents the path of least resistance."
~ Nischala Joy Devi

Off the Mat: Be mindful of what you do and why you do it in your daily life. Today you are creating tomorrow's legacy.

ℱocus: *Self-reflection*

Self-reflection is a wonderful way to become aware of the abundance in our lives, rather than the lack, as well as to learn about ourselves, our relationships, and what makes us truly happy and at peace. The *Naikan* ("Inside Looking") *Practice*, developed by Yoshimoto Ishin, a devout Buddhist monk, offers three insightful questions to answer honestly while sitting alone in a quiet place, looking within, without analyzing or judging ourselves or others.

1. *What have I received today?*
   Be aware of simple things like someone's smile, a bird's song, a polite act, etc. The motivation for the giving is not important. (Were you aware of feeling gratitude?)
2. *What have I given today?*
   Include the simple things like feeding your dog, sending a birthday card, making a call, etc.) Your motivation is irrelevant. (Were you aware of making a positive contribution to the planet?)
3. *What difficulties and troubles did I cause today?*
   Don't forget honking at someone, asking an embarrassing question, being short-tempered, etc. We are all too aware of how others cause us inconvenience or difficulty, but rarely notice when we do it.

On the Mat: Apply these three questions in relation to yourself through your practice today.

Awakening the Body: Looking within
- **Easy Seat** (Sukhasana), Stretches
- **Child's Pose** (Balasana)
- **Cat-Cow** (Marjaryasana), Twist
- **Downward Facing Dog** (Adho Mukha Svanasana)
- **Side Plank Pose** (Vasisthasana)
- **Downward Facing Dog** (Adho Mukha Svanasana)
- **Standing Forward Fold** (Uttanasana)

Standing
- **Mountain Pose** (Tedasana)
- **Sun Salutation** (Surya Namaskar)
  - **Runner's Lunge**
  - **Low Lunge** (Anjaneyasana)
  - **Plank Pose**
  - **Cobra Pose** (Bhujangasana)
  - **Plank Pose**
  - **Downward Facing Dog** (Adho Mukha Svanasana)
- **Yoga Mudra**

Mat
- **Thread the Needle**
- **Child's Pose** (Balasana)
- **Thunderbolt Pose** (Vajrasana), Twist
- **Bridge Pose** (Setu Bandha Sarvangasana)
- **Supine Twists**
- **Corpse Pose** (Savasana)

"Look within, and raise your awareness.
'Don't just do something, sit there!'"
~ Thich Nyat Hanh

Off the Mat: At the end of your day, reflect on the above three questions. Notice your actions, your reaction to your answers, and how this serves you in the days to come.

𝒢ocus: Full Integration of Body, Mind, and Breath

Full presence and commitment to our lives involves acting whole-heartedly in all our efforts, no matter how trivial they may seem. When our body, mind, and breath are fully engaged in the same activity, we experience peace and ease. Stress and dis-ease aren't caused by our circumstances as much as by this dis-integration, or 'fractured attention.'

Time disappears when you are in the midst of your favorite pastime, which may be reading, skiing, sports, dancing, or any other engaging activity. Then you are fully integrated, giving your all, and wholly in the moment.

"When a tiger catches a mouse, she does so with her full effort."
~ Eric Walrabenstein (Yogi E)

On the Mat: Focus totally on each step of the pose, then maintain the momentum of the ease you've created. Be completely in the moment.

Awakening the Body: Wholehearted attention
- **Cat-Cow** (Marjaryasana)
- **Gate Pose** (Parighasana) *Block*
- **Child's Pose** (Balasana)
- **Downward Facing Dog** (Adho Mukha Svanasana)
  - **Three-legged Dog**
  - **Fire Hydrant Pose**
- **Plank Pose**
- **Downward Facing Dog** (Adho Mukha Svanasana)
- **Standing Forward Fold** (Uttanasana)

Standing
- **Sun Salutation** (Surya Namaskar)
  - **Runner's Lunge**
  - **Downward Facing Dog** (Adho Mukha Svanasana)
- **Triangle Pose** (Trikonasana) *Block*
- **Wide-legged Forward Fold** (Prasarita Padottanasana)
  - Twist
  - **Yoga Mudra**

Mat
- **Bound Angle Pose** (Baddha Konasana)
- **Head to Knee Pose** (Janu Sirsasana)
- **Half Lord of the Fishes Pose** (Ardha Matsyendrasana)
- **Supine Twists**
- **Corpse Pose** (Savasana)

*"Optimally practiced, yoga is not about escaping
our lives, it's about transforming them."*
~ Eric Walrabenstein (Yogi E)

Off the Mat: The invitation is to bring your wholehearted attention to each activity in your day, noticing the level of fulfillment and ease that is created. Catch even the smallest mouse with your full effort.

Lesson Eighteen

𝒥ocus: Gratitude

There is an old Sufi story about a man whose son captured a strong, beautiful, wild horse, and all the neighbors told the man how fortunate he was. The man patiently replied, "We will see." One day the horse threw the son, who broke his leg, and all the neighbors told the man how cursed he was that the son had ever found the horse. Again the man answered, "We will see." Soon after the son broke his leg, soldiers came to the village and took away all the able-bodied young men, but because of the leg, the son was spared. When the man's friends told him how lucky the broken leg was, the man would only say, "We will see."

We don't know what result will come from our actions each day, so we can practice gratitude for participating in the mystery of life, and just be open and say, "We will see."

"The understanding you gain from practicing gratitude frees you from being lost or identified with either the negative or the positive aspects of life, letting you simply meet life in each moment as it arises."
~ Phillip Moffitt

On the Mat: Be consciously grateful for having made the wise choice to practice yoga and for being physically able to do as much as you are doing today.

Awakening the Body: Gratitude for whatever arises
- **Easy Seat** (Sukhasana), Stretches *Strap*
  - o **Yoga Mudra**
  - o **Cow Face Pose,** Arms (Gomukhasana)
- **Child's Pose** (Balasana)
- **Hands and Knees,** Twist
- **Downward Facing Dog** (Adho Mukha Svanasana)
- **Plank Pose**
- **Side Plank Pose** (Vasisthasana)
- **Downward Facing Dog** (Adho Mukha Svanasana)
- **Standing Forward Fold** (Uttanasana)
  - o **Big Toe Pose** (Padangusthasana)

Standing
- **Half Sun Salutation** (Ardha Surya Namaskar)
- **Chair Pose** (Uttkatasana)
- **Warrior I** (Virabhadrasana I)   ⎫
- **Intense Side Stretch** (Parsvottanasana) *Blocks* ⎬
- **Standing Forward Fold** (Uttanasana)   ⎭

Mat
- **Seated Forward Fold** (Paschimottanasana), Twist
- **Seated Half Happy Baby** (Ardha Ananda Balasana)
- **Supine Twists**
- **Corpse Pose** (Savasana)

"In everything give thanks."
~ Paul, the Apostle

Off the Mat: Notice: Do you experience the positive things in your life in true proportion to the negative things, or do the bad things receive a disproportionate amount of your attention, such that you have a distorted sense of your life?

Lesson Nineteen

𝒥ocus: **Letting go** — Pain vs. Suffering

There is a Zen story of two monks who were once traveling together down a muddy road. A heavy rain was falling. Coming around a bend, they met a lovely girl in a silk kimono and sash, unable to cross the intersection. "Come on, girl," said the first monk. Lifting her in his arms, he carried her over the mud. The second monk did not speak again until that night when they reached a lodging temple. Then he no longer could restrain himself. "We monks don't go near females," he said. "It is dangerous. Why did you do that?" "I left the girl there," the first monk said. "Are you still carrying her?"

Pain is the reality of the situation around us, but suffering is caused by our relationship to that reality. We don't always have control of the objective reality, but we can control our attitude toward it. Detach from the pain, whether from the past or the present, by letting it go and staying in the present moment. Access your breath and focus on this moment, then this, then this…

On the 𝔐at: Practice letting go of old, preconceived notions of what you can and cannot do in each pose. Stay in this moment, as though each movement is a first time for you.

Awakening the Body: Let go of past notions
- **Thunderbolt Pose** (Vajrasana), Stretches, Fold
- **Cat-Cow**, Twist
- **Child's Pose** (Balasana)
- **Downward Facing Dog** (Adho Mukha Svanasana)
- **Standing Forward Fold** (Uttanasana)

Standing
- **Standing Stretches**
- **Warrior II** (Virabhadrasana II)
- **Reverse Warrior** }
- **Side Angle Pose** (Utthita Parsvakonasana) }
- **Triangle Pose** (Trikonasana) *Block*
- **Eagle Pose** (Garudasana)
- **Yoga Mudra**

Mat
- **Bound Angle Pose** (Baddha Konasana), Twist, Fold
- **Bridge Pose** (Setu Bandha Sarvangasana) *Block*
- **Supine Twists**
- **Corpse Pose** (Savasana)

> *"The way to catch a monkey in India is to drop a handful of nuts into a jar with a small opening. The monkey puts his hand into the jar, grabs the nuts, and then finds that he can't get his fist out through the opening.*
>
> *If the monkey would just let go of the nuts, he could escape, but he won't.*
>
> *Conclusion: Attachment leads to suffering. Detachment leads to freedom."*
>
> ~ Ram Dass

Off the Mat: The Buddha said, "What you will be is what you do now." Let go of the past, which is anything before this moment. Why are you "…still carrying her [worry, resentment, pain, judgment, anger, etc.]?"

Focus: *Ragah* and *Dveshah* — Attachment and Aversion

The *Yoga Sutras* tell us that *"Happiness is like the musk deer. The musk deer has a scented spot above its forehead that gives off the musk fragrance. This deer runs here and there in search of the scent, not knowing the scent comes from its own forehead."*
~ Patanjali, II:7,8

We attach ourselves to the things outside of ourselves that bring us pleasure (*Sukha*), and create aversions to those things that bring us unhappiness (*Dhukha*), without realizing that happiness is already within us. No one or no thing can give this to us, but can only reflect or distort our own, inner self.

Don't be like the little deer running all over looking for your happiness and peace outside of yourself. Know that it comes from within.

On the Mat: Though our happiness is already in us, it often needs to be accessed through self-reflection and acute awareness of the moment. Set an intention that your inner peace during your practice will not be contingent upon your performance on the mat.

Awakening the Body: Inner peace in the midst of challenge

- **Easy Seat** (Sukhasana), Stretches *Block*
- **Child's Pose** (Balasana)
- **Dolphin Pose**
- **Child's Pose** (Balasana)
- **Downward Facing Dog** (Adho Mukha Svanasana)
- **Standing Forward Fold** (Uttanasana)

Standing

- **Half Sun Salutation** (Ardha Surya Namaskar)
- **Warrior I** (Virabhadrasana I)
- **Warrior III** (Virabhadrasana III)
- **Intense Side Stretch** (Parsvottanasana) *Blocks*
- **Cow Face Pose** (Gomukhasana) *Strap*
- **Yoga Mudra**
- **Standing Forward Fold** (Uttanasana)

Mat

- **Boat Pose** (Navasana)
- **Easy Seat**, Forward Fold
- **Marichi's Twist** (Marichyasana III)
- **Bound Angle Pose** (Baddha Konasana)
- **Supine Twists**
- **Corpse Pose** (Savasana)

"Everything that irritates us about others can lead us to an understanding of ourselves."

~ Carl Jung

Off the Mat: There is no need to look any further than within your own heart for the happiness you are seeking. Notice what is reflected back at you from others during your day.

Lesson Twenty-One

𝓕ocus: *Pratipaksha Bhavanam* — Opposite Thoughts

Yoga is very realistic in identifying the strengths and frailties of humankind. Knowing that negative thoughts are a natural part of the mind, the *Yoga Sutras* helps us to deal with them in our quest toward happiness by guiding the mind to act in accordance with the yogic ideals of the *Yamas* and the *Niyamas*. Some of these practical suggestions include: inviting opposite thoughts, changing one's environment, thinking of the possible consequences, and breaking the negative cycle through distractions. By reflection on our thoughts, words, and deeds, we are given the chance to move from reacting to choosing.

> *"When disturbed by negative thoughts, opposite (positive)*
> *ones should be thought of. This is pratipaksha bhavana."*
> ~ Patanjali, *Yoga Sutras* II:33

On the 𝓜at: Be aware of any negative thoughts you have about yourself or your performance during your asana practice.

Awakening the Body: Removing negativity and tension in the hips
- **Child's Pose** (Balasana)
- **Plank Pose**
- **Downward Facing Dog** (Adho Mukha Svanasana)
- **Runner's Lunge**
- **Low Lunge** (Anjaneyasana)
- **Child's Pose** (Balasana)
- **Downward Facing Dog** (Adho Mukha Svanasana)
  - **Plank Pose**
  - **Pigeon Pose** (Eka Pada Rajakapotasana)
  - **Three-legged Dog**
  - **Fire Hydrant Pose**
- **Standing Forward Fold** (Uttanasana)

Standing
- **Half Sun Salutation** (Ardha Surya Namaskar)
- **Warrior II** (Virabhadrasana II)
- **Reverse Warrior**
- **Side Angle Pose** (Parsvakonasana)
- **Standing Forward Fold** (Uttanasana)

Mat
- **Bound Angle Pose** (Baddha Konasana), Twist
- **Figure Four Stretch**
- **Bound Angle Pose**, Lifted
- **Supine Twists**
- **Corpse Pose** (Savasana)

"These disturbing thoughts that consume us at times arise from our past. They are based in fears and hurts from our past experiences. Pratipaksha Bhavana gives us a concrete methodology that we can use to begin addressing and changing these damaging patterns."
~ TKV Desikachar

Off the Mat: During your day, notice any negative thoughts that might arise. Practice replacing them with (opposite) positive ones, and see how you feel. As a measuring stick, ask yourself, "How does this serve me now?"

$\mathcal{F}$ocus: **Receiving** — Making Space in Order to Receive

There are people who love to give of themselves to others, while not allowing others to give to them, feeling perhaps vulnerable if they do. However, aren't you depriving others from getting the pleasure that comes from giving and helping, if you aren't able to receive graciously from them?

In the same vein, are you refusing to allow the universe to give to you if you feel that you don't deserve the good things that are being offered?

The first *"paramita"*, or *"perfect realization"*, taught by the Buddha is *"dana paramita"* — giving, offering, and generosity. I would add that it includes your allowance of others to give to you, as well as giving to yourself.

> *"Whether you give your presence, your stability, your freshness, your solidity, your freedom, or your understanding, your gift can work a miracle. Dana paramita is the practice of love."*
> ~ Thich Nhat Hanh

On the Mat: Open your heart, making room to receive love and truth. While quiet, distinguish between the chatty mind and your true inner voice, and be ready to believe what you hear. Give and receive mindfully.

Awakening the Body: Open and receive, from yourself and others

- **Reclining Bound Angle Pose** (Supta Baddha Konasana) *Blankets, Blocks*
- **Reclining Big Toe Pose** (Supta Padangusthasana) *Strap*
- **Child's Pose** (Balasana) *Block*
- **Forward Twist** *Blankets*
- **Child's Pose** (Balasana)
- **Downward Facing Dog** (Adho Mukha Svanasana)
- **Standing Forward Fold** (Uttanasana)

Standing
- **Warrior I** (Virabhadrasana I), arms wide, heart open
- **Intense Side Stretch Pose** (Parsvottanasana) *Blocks*
- **Wide-legged Forward Fold** (Prasarita Padottanasana) *Block*
- **Standing Side Stretches**
- **Yoga Mudra**

Mat
- **Bound Angle Pose** (Baddha Konasana), Fold
- **Bridge Pose** (Setu Bandha Sarvangasana) *Block*
- **Supine Twists**
- **Corpse Pose** (Savasana)

"The less you open your heart to others,
the more your heart suffers."
~ Deepak Chopra

Off the Mat: Set an intention to allow others to participate in your life, to get pleasure from giving to You, and graciously receive that show of love with an open heart.

Focus: Peace in the Midst of Chaos

Sitting within the eye of a storm is a good analogy for finding a place of peace in the midst of possible chaos around us. The heavens rage while within the center, there is calm and detachment. Likewise, when things don't turn out as we've planned, when results don't meet expectations, or when people are trying to do too many things at once, by stepping back into 'witness consciousness' and letting go of all "supposed to be's", we can reconnect to breath and find our place of peace. Remembering that discontent arises from wanting things to be other than they are at that moment, we can embrace what is now, and let go of expectations.

"In detachment lies the wisdom of uncertainty...
in the wisdom of uncertainty lies the freedom
from our past, from the known,
which is the prison of past conditioning.

And in our willingness to step into the
unknown, the field of all possibilities,
we surrender ourselves to the creative mind
that orchestrates the dance of the universe."
~ Deepak Chopra

On the Mat: The practice of "Four-Corner Awareness" allows everything in the room to be in our field of awareness spontaneously and equally. Visualize the four corners of the room and everything in it, without looking *through* the mind, but rather *at* the mind as one more thing in our awareness.

Awakening the Body: Each pose within Four-Corner Awareness
- On back, pelvic tilts, lifts, arms in vinyasa with breath
- **Happy Baby** (Ananda Balasana)
- **Easy Seat** (Sukhasana), Fold
- **Child's Pose** (Balasana)
- **Side Plank Pose** (Vasisthasana)
- **Child's Pose** (Balasana)
- **Downward Facing Dog** (Adho Mukha Svanasana)
- **Standing Forward Fold** (Uttanasana)
    - **Big Toe Pose** (Padangusthasana)
    - **Wrist Stretch** (Padahasthasana)

Standing
- **Mountain Pose** (Tedasana)
- **Standing Stretches**, arms in vinyasa with breath
- **Eagle Pose** (Garudasana)
- **Yoga Mudra**
- **Standing Forward Fold** (Uttanasana)
    - Twist

Mat
- **Seated Forward Fold** (Paschimottanasana)
- **Head to Knee Pose** (Janu Sirsasana), Twist
- **Supine Twists**
- **Corpse Pose** (Savasana)

"For us, there is only the trying. The rest is not our business."
~ T.S. Eliot

Off the Mat: Deal with what is, not with what should be. Therein lies the eye of the storm.

ℱocus: "Which Wolf Will You Feed?"

"One evening an old Cherokee told his grandson about a battle that goes on inside people. He said, 'My son, the battle is between two wolves inside us all.

One is Evil (Unhappiness). It is anger, envy, jealousy, sorrow, regret, greed, arrogance, self-pity, guilt, resentment, inferiority, lies, false pride, superiority, and ego.

The other is Good (Happiness). It is joy, peace, love, hope, serenity, humility, kindness, benevolence, empathy, generosity, truth, compassion, and faith.'

The grandson thought about it for a minute and then asked his grandfather: 'Which wolf wins?'

The old Cherokee simply replied, 'The one you feed.'"

~ Cherokee Indian legend

On the Mat: Will you be negative and critical of your performance and possible limitations in the poses, or positive and accepting of whatever arises? Which wolf will you feed?

Awakening the Body: Equal and opposite energy

Standing
- **Standing Stretches**
- **Sun Salutation** (Surya Namaskar)
  - **Runner's Lunge**
  - **Low Lunge** (Anjaneyasana)
  - **Chair Pose** (Uttkatasana)
- **Mountain Pose** (Tedasana)
- **Warrior II** (Virabhadrasana II) ⎫
- **Side Angle Pose** (Parsvakonasana) ⎬
- **Triangle Pose** (Trikonasana) ⎫
- **Reverse Triangle** ⎬
- **Standing Forward Fold** (Uttanasana)

Mat
- **Child's Pose** (Balasana)
- **Cat-Cow** (Marjaryasana)
- **Thunderbolt Pose** (Vajrasana), with back bend
- **Seated Forward Fold** (Paschimottanasana)
- **Supine Twists**
- **Corpse Pose** (Savasana)

> *"We must make the choices that enable us to fulfill
> the deepest capacities of our real selves."*
> ~ Thomas Merton

Off the Mat: Each day you have the choice whether to feed the evil wolf or the good wolf, of living by the *yamas* and *niyamas*, or ignoring them. Which wolf will you feed?

𝒢ocus: Finding *Santosha* — Unconditional Contentment

Yoga is about unconditional happiness, independent of the circumstances. It's about happiness Now, not "when I lose weight," or "when I get a better job," or "when I find a partner." It's about finding happiness within ourselves, and not relying upon outside people, objects, or activities for our happiness, like chocolate, shopping, or doing only the poses we like and can do easily.

In a yoga class I attended, there was a young student who kept moving her mat from the front to the back, from the right side to the left, asking if it was alright to move. The teacher simply smiled at her and said:

> *"Life goes with you no matter where you sit."*
> ~ Jane Gleason

On the Mat: Connecting to your breath keeps you in the Now at every moment, in every pose. Just this, on this mat, in this space, right here, right now.

Awakening the Body: Breath keeps you present
- **Thunderbolt Pose** (Vajrasana), Stretches *Strap*
- **Gate Pose** (Parighasana) *Block*
- **Child's Pose** (Balasana)
- **Downward Facing Dog** (Adho Mukha Svanasana)
- **Standing Forward Fold** (Uttanasana), Twist

Standing
- **Half Sun Salutation** (Ardha Surya Namaskar)
- **Mountain Pose** (Tedasana)
- **Upward Salute** (Urdhva Hastasana)
- **Tree Pose** (Vrksasana)
- **Yoga Mudra**
- **Chair Pose** (Uttkatasana), Twist
- **Standing Forward Fold** (Uttanasana)

Mat
- **Cow Face Pose** (Gomukhasana) *Strap*
- **Bound Angle Pose** (Baddha Konasana), Twist
- **Supine Twists**
- **Corpse Pose** (Savasana)

"Wherever you go, there you are."
~ Jon Kabat-Zinn

Off the Mat: During your day, notice if you put off happiness, waiting for it to come from an external source. One thing is for certain: "Life goes with you no matter where you sit."

Lesson Twenty-Six

Focus: Sankalpas — Intentions

How did the New Year's resolution and 'Starting on Monday' devolve from a change for the better into an exercise in self-criticism? Lose 10 pounds says, "I'm fat"; eat more fruits and veggies says, "I'm unhealthy"; remember to call someone weekly says, "I'm ungrateful."

From now on, set a *"Sankulpa"*, an intention, a resolution with a yogic twist. Instead of feeling guilty or angry at yourself if you "fail," explore what's behind the thought or feeling or desire and be softer with yourself. Praise the nobility of the effort, rather than focusing on what you're doing wrong.

> *"If your compassion does not include yourself, it is incomplete."*
> ~ The Buddha

On the Mat: Set an intention for your morning, your day, your year. Be kind, encouraging, and loving to yourself during your practice on the mat. Detach from the result, let it go…Trust in the inherent wisdom of nature.

Awakening the Body: With kindness
- **Reclined Bound Angle** (Supta Baddha Konasana) *Blanket, Blocks*
- **Reclined Big Toe Pose** (Supta Padangusthasana) *Strap*
- **Cat-Cow** (Marjaryasana), Twist
- **Child's Pose** (Balasana)
- **Downward Facing Dog** (Adho Mukha Svanasana)
- **Standing Forward Fold** (Uttanasana)

Standing
- **Sun Salutation** (Surya Namaskar)
  - **Low Lunge** (Anjaneyasana)
  - **Plank Pose**
  - **Cobra** (Bhujangasana)
  - **Downward Facing Dog** (Adho Mukha Svanasana)
- **Standing Forward Fold** (Uttanasana), Twist

Mat
- **Child's Pose** (Balasana)
- **Seated Forward Fold** (Paschimottanasana)
- **Bridge** (Setu Bandha Sarvangasana)
- **Supine Twists**
- **Corpse Pose** (Savasana)

"Nature is such a beautiful example of non-attachment. Notice how the earth changes with the seasons, never holding on to one longer than the other. Trees bud in the spring and their leaves grow to fullness in the summer. They let go of their leaves in the fall to stand naked in the winter months only to repeat the cycle. There is an inherent wisdom in nature, a trust that goes beyond attachment. If we can achieve this greedless state and trust in our higher nature, then we, too, can know the wisdom of trusting the unknown."
~ Author unknown

Off the Mat: Set your *Sankalpas*. Look inward through journaling and meditating. Question your usual resolutions and how they make you feel, then reframe them into softer intentions. Be firm but fair with yourself. If you stray from your *Sankalpa*, don't berate yourself. Gently remind yourself by using it as your mantra or posting it on your mirror.

Lesson Twenty-Seven

ℱocus: **Equanimity**

In the *Bhagavad Gita* it is written, *"Sammatwam yoga uchathe"* — "The goal of yoga is balance." *"Sammatwam"* in other contexts also means moderation and equanimity, bringing the body, mind, and spirit into balance.

In the words of teacher Sharon Salzberg, equanimity is *"a spacious stillness of the mind, a radiant calm that allows us to be present fully with all the different changing experiences that constitute our world and our lives."* As we experience the full range of human emotions, yoga teaches us to let go of our attachments to things being a certain way for ourselves and others, while we continue to strive for the best.

> *"If your mind becomes firm like a rock*
> *And no longer shakes*
> *In a world where everything is shaking,*
> *Your mind will be your greatest friend*
> *And suffering will not come your way."*
> ~ The Theragatha, Verses of the Elder Monks

On the Mat: Through mindful breathing and movements, we can access a place of calm within us amidst the distraction of screaming muscles and distracting thoughts.

Awakening the Body: Finding the calm within
- **Thunderbolt Pose** (Vajrasana), neck and shoulder stretches
- **Cat-Cow** (Marjaryasana)
- **Child's Pose** (Balasana)
- **Downward Facing Dog** (Adho Mukha Svanasana)
- **Plank**
- **Side Plank Pose** (Vasisthasana) *Blocks*
- **Downward Facing Dog** (Adho Mukha Svanasana)
- **Standing Forward Fold** (Uttanasana)
    - **Big Toe Pose** (Padangusthasana)
    - **Twist**

Standing
- **Standing Stretches**
- **Triangle Pose** (Trikonasana)
- **Reverse Triangle**
- **Wide-legged Forward Fold** (Prasarita Padottanasana)
    - **Yoga Mudra** (First Side)
    - **Twist** (Second Side)
- **Standing Forward Fold** (Uttanasana)

Mat
- **Camel Pose** (Ustrasana) *Blocks*
- **Child's Pose** (Balasana)
- **Head to Knee Forward Fold** (Janu Sirsasana)
- **Marichi's Twist** (Marichyasana)
- **Supine Twists**
- **Corpse Pose** (Savasana)

"One who eats and plays in moderation, who is moderate in sleeping and waking, and who is disciplined with their yoga practice, for such a person, yoga destroys all suffering."
~ Bhagavad Gita, VI:17

Off the Mat: You can't always control the reality of a situation, but you can decide your attitudes and responses to it. Choose to reconnect with breath and create a quiet place within to fortify yourself.

ℱocus: **Limited Thoughts Yield Limited Results**

Every day is an opportunity for new beginnings, new hopes and intentions, and you don't want to limit what you can accomplish by thinking limited thoughts.

During our yoga poses, thinking in words is often limiting because of our judgmental and labeling minds. One way to get out of your head is to just 'feel', to connect with breath and be aware of the tingling sensations, the places of discomfort or stiffness, the feelings of lightness or ease. As you move and breathe in your practice on the mat, your physical body becomes a vehicle to connect with yourself on a much deeper and more significant level. Just step out of your own way.

"Anytime you run into a wall or a closed door,
the first place to try to open it is in your own mind."
~ Author unknown

On the Mat: During your asana practice, feel every cell in your body, simultaneously, without words.

Awakening the Body: Don't think, feel
- **Child's Pose** (Balasana)
- **Extended Puppy Pose** (Uttana Shishosana)
- **Dolphin Pose**
- **Child's Pose** (Balasana)
- **Downward Facing Dog** (Adho Mukha Svanasana)
- **Standing Forward Fold** (Uttanasana)

Standing
- **Mountain Pose** (Tedasana)
- **Eagle Pose** (Garudasana)
- **Warrior II** (Virabhadrasana II)
- **Side Angle Pose** (Parsvakonasana)
- **Runner's Lunge**
- **Downward Facing Dog** (Adho Mukha Svanasana)
- **Standing Forward Fold** (Uttanasana)

Mat
- **Thread the Needle** *Blanket*
- **Child's Pose** (Balasana)
- **Bound Angle Pose** (Baddha Konasana)
- **Wide Angle Seated Forward Fold** (Upavistha Konasana)
- **Supine Twists**
- **Corpse Pose** (Savasana)

"As you think, so you become."
~ The Buddha

Off the Mat: During your day, avoid judgment and criticism, of yourself and others. Once you listen to and trust your own inner voice within that deep place of quiet, words will cease and feeling and clarity will remain.

Lesson Twenty-Nine

𝒥ocus: **The Yoga of Speech** — The Power of Words

Right Speech is one of the pillars of the Eightfold Path of the Buddha, raising our consciousness about the power and effect of our words. Through self-inquiry (*Svadyaya*), we can better understand the motivations, emotions, and thoughts behind our words. If you ask yourself the following questions, attributed to Sri Sathya Sai Baba, you give yourself time to consider your words before uttering them.

1. *Is it kind?*
2. *Is it true?*
3. *Is it necessary?*
4. *Does it improve on the silence?*

On the Mat: In each pose, find something kind and true to say to yourself. Let that truth resonate within your heart and absorb it.

Awakening the Body: Open up your heart
- **Reclining Bound Angle** (Supta Badha Konasana) *Blanket, Block*
- **Reclining Big Toe Pose** (Supta Padangusthasana) *Strap*
- **Child's Pose** (Balasana)
- **Downward Facing Dog** (Adho Mukha Svanasana)
- **Plank Pose**
- **Side Plank Pose** (Vasisthasana)
- **Downward Facing Dog** (Adho Mukha Svanasana)
- **Standing Forward Fold** (Uttanasana)

Standing
- **Half Sun Salutation** (Ardha Surya Namaskar)
- **Warrior I** (Virabhadrasana I)
- **Intense Side Stretch Pose** (Parsvottanasana) *Blocks*
- **Wide-legged Forward Fold** (Prasarita Padottanasana)
  - **Twist**

Mat
- **Staff Pose** (Dandasana)
- **Seated Forward Fold** (Paschimottanasana)
- **Upward Plank Pose** (Purvottanasana)
- **Bound Angle Pose** (Baddha Konasana), Fold
- **Bridge Pose** (Setu Banda Sarvangasana)
- **Supine Twists**
- **Corpse Pose** (Savasana)

"Speech that can change and inspire us, speech that resonates from our highest Self, comes out of our contact with the silent place behind the words, the place we reach when we're able to pause, turn into the heart, and let the stillness speak through our words. Speech that comes out of stillness is speech that comes, quite literally, from the source of wisdom itself."
~ Sally Kempton, Durgananda

Off the Mat: Throughout your day, continue "Right Speech", both when addressing yourself and others. Make note of how this serves you.

FOCUS: Yoga is the Stilling of the Fluctuations of the Mind.

~ Patanjali, *Yoga Sutras*, 1:2

Sitting in stillness, whether in meditation, prayer, or within asanas, gives us the opportunity to clear our minds of troublesome thoughts, to stay in the present as we connect to breath, to let go of thinking and doing and surrender to the silence and peace already within us, to hear the inner voice of our truth.

"Ten thousand flowers in spring,
the moon in autumn,
a cool breeze in summer,
snow in winter.

If your mind isn't clouded
by unnecessary things,
this is the best season of your life."

~ Wu Men

On the Mat: Notice what fluctuations distract your mind. Return to breath and stay in just this moment...then this...then this.

Awakening the Body: Quieting the mind
- **Easy Seat** (Sukhasana), with Sama-Vritti (Equal Breaths)
- **Cat-Cow** (Marjaryasana)
- **Child's Pose** (Balasana)
- **Gate Pose** (Parighasana) *Block*
- **Downward Facing Dog** (Adho Mukha Svanasana)
- **Standing Forward Fold** (Uttanasana)

Standing
- **Warrior I** (Virabhadrasana I)
- **Warrior II** (Virabhadrasana II)
- **Side Angle Pose** (Parsvakonasana)
- **Chair Pose** (Uttkatasana)
- **Mountain Pose** (Tedasana)
- **Upward Salute** (Urdhva Hastasana)
- **Standing Forward Fold** (Uttanasana)

Mat
- **Cow Face Pose** (Gomukhasana) *Strap*
- **Seated Forward Fold** (Paschimottanasana), Twist
- **Supine Twists**

*"See how nature — trees, flowers, grass — grows in silence;
see the stars, the moon and the sun, how they move in
silence...We need silence to be able to touch souls."*
~ Mother Teresa

Off the Mat: Give yourself the gift of silence regularly and notice
how this affects your insights, attitudes, and behavior.

Focus: The Ego is a Monkey

Whereas the heart or inner voice whispers, the ego loudly yells, making demands throughout our day in the form of "I want." Pulling back into Witness Consciousness allows us to observe more objectively who and what we are in relation to the stage of the world, taking us from the limited self (your name) to the expansive Self (I am).

"The ego is a monkey catapulting through the jungle:
Totally fascinated by the realm of the senses,
* it swings from one desire to the next,*
* one conflict to the next,*
* one self-centered idea to the next.*
If you threaten it, it actually fears for its life.

Let this monkey go.
Let the senses go.
Let desires go.
Let conflicts go.
Let ideas go.
Let the fiction of life and death go.
Just remain in the center, watching.

And then forget that you are there."
~ Lao Tzu, from the *Hua Hu Ching*

On the Mat: Find the quiet, calm place inside of the "I am" as you practice your asanas and ignore the demands of the ego crying out for your attention. Step back into Witness Consciousness, "…and then forget that you are there."

Awakening the Body: Forget that you are there
- **Thunderbolt Pose** (Vajrasana), Stretches
- **Table-Top**, arm and leg balance
- **Child's Pose** (Balasana)
- **Dolphin Pose**
- **Child's Pose** (Balasana)
- **Downward Facing Dog** (Adho Mukha Svanasana)
  - **Three-legged Dog**
  - **Fire Hydrant Pose**
- **Standing Forward Fold** (Uttanasana)

Standing
- **Mountain Pose** (Tedasana)
- **Surya Namaskar** (Sun Salutation)
  - **Runner's Lunge**, with Twist
- **Upward Salute** (Urdhva Hastasana)
- **Tree Pose** (Vrksasana)
- **Cow Face Pose** (Gomukhasana) *Strap*
- **Yoga Mudra**

Mat
- **Boat Pose** (Navasana)
- **Head to Knee Pose** (Janu Sirsasana)
- **Easy Seat** (Sukhasana), Fold, Twist
- **Supine Twists**
- **Corpse Pose** (Savasana)

*"Letting go of the [ego]…and letting go of the mind open
the possibility of experiencing an aspect of your being that is
beyond your usual limitations. This is the realm of spirit."*
~ Deepak Chopra

Off the Mat: Throughout your day, ignore the yelling of the ego
and realize it is fighting for its life. Listen closely to the whispers
of the heart for guidance…"Then forget that you are there."

Lesson Thirty-Two

*F*ocus: **Smiling is Infectious**

A smile goes a long way. Have you noticed that it's more difficult to stay depressed or angry if you even force yourself to smile? That generally people will reflect your smile right back at you like a mirror, or that perhaps you have that response to others? Your smile may be the only sunshine for someone in their otherwise dreary day.

"If we are peaceful, if we are happy, we can smile
and blossom like a flower, and everyone in our family,
our entire society, will benefit from our peace."
~ Thich Nhat Hanh, *Being Peace*

On the Mat: Put on a smile as you go through your poses today and see how this affects your body and your mind.

Awakening the Body: Smile
- **Bound Angle Pose** (Baddha Konasana), Stretches
- **Lion's Pose** (Simhasana)
- **Gate Pose** (Parighasana)
- **Child's Pose** (Balasana)
- **Downward Facing Dog** (Adho Mukha Svanasana)
- **Standing Forward Fold** (Uttanasana)

Standing
- **Sun Salutation** (Surya Namaskar)
  - **Low Lunge** (Anjaneyasana)
  - **Plank**
  - **Cobra** (Bhujangasana)
  - **Plank**
  - **Downward Facing Dog** (Adho Mukha Svanasana)
- **Triangle Pose** (Trikonasana)
  - Clasp hands behind back
- **Reverse Triangle**
  - Clasp hands behind back
- **Yoga Mudra**

Mat
- **Thread the Needle**
- **Child's Pose** (Balasana)
- **Easy Seat** (Sukhasana), Twist, Fold
- **Supine Twists**
- **Corpse Pose** (Savasana)

*"A smile is the light in the window of your face
that tells people you're at home."*
~ Author unknown

Off the Mat: As an experiment, smile throughout your day, both at others and to yourself, and see how this affects your experience of peace and happiness.

Focus: Impartial and Non-judgmental

We are usually our own worst critics, feeding and pampering the demands of our ego selves. Yoga teaches us that non-judgment is the key to inner peace and satisfying relationships. Yoga teaches us to deal with what is, not with what we prefer it to be.

"Heaven and earth are impartial; they see the 10,000 things as straw dogs.
The sage is not sentimental; he treats all his people as straw dogs.

The sage is like heaven and earth:
To him none are especially dear, nor is there anyone he disfavors.
He gives and gives, without condition, offering his treasures to everyone.

Between heaven and earth is a space like a bellows;
empty and inexhaustible, the more it is used, the more it produces.

Hold on to the center.
Man was made to sit quietly and find the truth within."
~ Lao Tzu, Tao Te Ching, Fifth Verse

On the Mat: Repeat this intention: "I eliminate all of my judgments of others and of myself." Using Witness Consciousness, detach from your false ego self and observe your performance impartially and without judgment.

Awakening the Body: Impartial as heaven and earth
- **Thunderbolt Pose** (Vajrasana), Stretches *Strap*
- **Cat-Cow** (Marjaryasana), Twist
- **Downward Facing Dog** (Adho Mukha Svanasana)
- **Standing Forward Fold** (Uttanasana)
  - **Big Toe Pose** (Padangusthasana)
  - **Wrist Stretch** (Padahastasana)

Standing
- **Standing Stretches**
- **Tree Pose** (Vrksasana)
- **Intense Side Stretch** (Parsvottanasana) *Blocks* }
- **Revolved Triangle** *Block*
- **Eagle Pose** (Garudasana)
- **Yoga Mudra**

Mat
- **Noose Pose** (Pasasana) *Blanket* under heels
- **Bound Angle Pose** (Baddha Konasana), Fold, Twist
- **Half Lord of the Fishes Pose** (Ardha Matsyendrasana)
- **Supine Twists**
- **Corpse Pose** (Savasana)

"Let's trade in all our judging for appreciating. Let's lay down our righteousness and just be together."
~ Ram Dass

Off the Mat: Fortunately, we have our laboratory on the mat, our place to notice our reactions and thoughts, but if we do not carry our practice beyond our asanas, we have missed out on the most valuable part of the lesson. Repeat your intention as a mantra: "I eliminate all of my judgments of others and of myself."

ℱocus: **Positive Thinking**

"Once upon a time in ancient China, there were two brothers. Both worked hard and accumulated much wealth. One day, they were traveling on a road when it started to rain. They found shelter in an abandoned temple at a nearby cemetery. An old man was already inside, holding a small gong in one hand and they asked him about it. The old man said: "I am a messenger. My job is to go to the door of people who are about to die and strike this gong three times, as the signal for them to pass away." He told the brothers that they would see for themselves the following week, as they must die at that time. And he vanished.

The older brother was very upset. He kept thinking that he worked hard to accumulate his wealth and didn't want to let it go. He lost his appetite for the worry and couldn't sleep. He soon became sick. On the appointed day, he heard the sound of the gong being struck three times and he died, as the old man had said.

The younger brother also thought about how hard he had worked for his wealth, but thought that he now had no time to waste to divest his possessions. He passed out his wealth generously to people and causes and the people got together to celebrate the good man with music and dancing. There was much gratitude and merriment and when the old man showed up, no one heard the three gongs. He tried over and over, to no avail, and finally just left in frustration. A week later, the brother wondered about the man with the gong, but then shrugged his shoulders and continued his good works."

~ *The Gong* Adapted from Derek Lin, *The Tao of Daily Life*

On the Mat: Practice being aware of your habits. Do you look at the negative or the positive in yourself? In the world? In others? Do you make the most of a situation?

Awakening the Body: Invigoration and celebration

- **Easy Seat** (Sukhasana), **Skull Brightening Breath** (Kapalabhati)
- **Child's Pose** (Balasana)
- **Downward Facing Dog** (Adho Mukha Svanasana)
  o Twist
- **Standing Forward Fold** (Uttanasana)

Standing

- **Sun Salutation** (Surya Namascar)
  o **Runner's Lunge**
  o **Plank Pose**, with push-ups
  o **Cobra** (Bhujangasana)
- **Warrior II** (Virabhadrasana II)
- **Reverse Warrior**
- **Side Angle Pose** (Parsvakonasana)
- **Yoga Mudra**

Mat

- **Child's Pose** (Balasana)
- **Bridge Pose** (Setu Bandha Sarvangasana)
- **Supine Twists**
- **Corpse Pose** (Savasana) (Extended time)

"The more you praise and celebrate your life,
the more there is in life to celebrate."
~ Oprah Winfrey

Off the Mat: Throughout your day, repeat the affirmation, "I celebrate life". Smile at people. Notice their response to you and how this affects your behavior and attitude.

Lesson Thirty-Five

𝔉ocus: **Comparing Ourselves to Others** — We are One

We are all part of a greater whole and are inextricably connected to one another.

> *"There was once a small wave who was unhappy. 'I'm so miserable,' it moaned. 'The other waves are big and powerful, while I'm so little and weak. Why is life so unfair?'*
>
> *Another wave passing by heard the small wave and decided to stop by. 'You only think so because you haven't seen your own original nature clearly. You think you're a wave and you think you're suffering. In reality you are neither.'*
>
> *'What?' The small wave was surprised. 'I'm not a wave? But it's obvious I'm a wave! I've got my crest, see? And there's my wake, little as it is. What do you mean I'm not a wave?'*
>
> *'The thing you call 'wave' is merely a temporary form you assume for a short time. You're really just water! When you understand completely that this is your fundamental nature, you will no longer be confused about being a wave, and you will be free of your misery.'*
>
> *'If I'm water, what about you?'*
>
> *'I'm water too. I'm temporarily assuming the form of a wave somewhat larger than you, but that doesn't change my fundamental essence…water! I'm you and you're me. We're part of a greater self.'"*
>
> *~ A Conversation of Waves* Adapted from Derek Lin, *The Tao of Daily Life*

On the 𝔐at: The invitation is to use the "So Ham" mantra, "I am that…," while connecting with breath.

Awakening the Body: So Ham…I am That
- **Reclined Big Toe Pose** (Supta Padangusthasana) *Strap*
- **Bound Angle Pose** (Baddha Konasana), Twist
- **Cat-Cow** (Marjaryasana), alternate arm-leg stretches
- **Gate Pose** (Parighasana) *Block*
- **Child's Pose** (Balasana)
- **Downward Facing Dog** (Adho Mukha Svanasana)
- **Standing Forward Fold** (Uttanasana)

Standing
- **Standing Stretches**
- **Warrior I** (Virabhadrasana I)
- **Warrior III** (Virabhadrasana III) *Block* }
- **Chair Pose** (Uttkatasana), Twist
- **Standing Forward Fold** (Uttanasana)

Mat
- **Plank Pose**
- **Pigeon Pose** (Eka Pada Rajakapotasana) *Blanket*
- **Downward Facing Dog** (Adho Mukha Svanasana)
- **Child's Pose** (Balasana)
- **Seated Forward Fold** (Paschimottanasana)
- **Head to Knee Pose** (Janu Sirsasana)
- **Supine Twists**
- **Corpse Pose** (Savasana)

"To discover joy is to return to a state of oneness with the universe."
~ Peggy Jenkins

Off the Mat: During your day, try repeating the affirmation, "I am part of a greater whole, a greater self." Notice how this affects your attitude and behavior.

esson Thirty-Six

ℱocus: **The Treasure Lies Inside of You**

People look outside of themselves for satisfaction, love, and happiness, when the treasure is within them all along. When things go wrong in our lives, we tend to regard the situation itself as the problem, but in reality, whatever problems we experience come from our attitudes and responses to that situation. Happiness is a state of mind; therefore, the real source of that feeling of abundance lies within the mind, not in external circumstances.

"A beggar had been sitting by the side of a road for over thirty years. One day a stranger walked by. "Spare some change?" mumbled the beggar, mechanically holding out his old baseball cap. "I have nothing to give you," said the stranger. Then he asked: "What's that you are sitting on?" "Nothing," replied the beggar. "Just an old box. I have been sitting on it for as long as I can remember." "Ever look inside?" asked the stranger. "No," said the beggar. "What's the point? There's nothing in there." "Have a look inside," insisted the stranger. The beggar managed to pry open the lid. With astonishment, disbelief, and elation, he saw that the box was filled with gold."

~ Eckhardt Tolle, *The Power of Now*

On the Mat: During your practice, listen to the inner voice in your heart for guidance in doing the poses safely for your body as it is in the moment. Set an affirmation to trust that voice, then notice how this serves you.

Awakening the Body: Listening within
- **Easy Seat** (Sukhasana), Breathe, visualize, connect with the heart
- **Reclined Bound Angle** (Supta Badha Konasana) *Blanket*
- Mindful Alternate-leg Bicycle Pumping
- **Child's Pose** (Balasana)
- **Extended Puppy Pose** (Uttana Shishosana)
- **Downward Facing Dog** (Adho Mukha Svanasana)
- **Standing Forward Fold** (Uttanasana)

Standing
- **Mountain Pose** (Tedasana)
- **Eagle Pose** (Garudasana)
- **Half Sun Salutation** (Ardha Surya Namaskar), heart opening
- **Wide-legged Forward Fold** (Prasarita Padottanasana)
  - Twist (First Side)
  - **Yoga Mudra** (Second Side)
- **Standing Forward Fold** (Uttanasana)

Mat
- **Staff Pose** (Dandasana), Twist
- **Upward Plank Pose** (Purvottanasana)
- **Supine Twists**
- **Corpse Pose** (Savasana), Extended

"One of the greatest moments in anybody's developing experience is when he no longer tries to hide from himself, but determines to get acquainted with himself as he really is."
~ Norman Vincent Peale

Off the Mat: During your day, ask questions of yourself, then listen to the inner voice in your heart for the answer. Set an affirmation to trust that voice, then notice how this serves you.

Lesson Thirty-Seven

Focus: Enjoying the Moment...TGINow

TGIF is actually a rather negative concept. What about Monday, Tuesday, etc? TGIF implies that each day is spent waiting for it to be Friday and is not enjoyed for its own sake. If we declare: "I won't be happy until...," then we're never in the moment, are always postponing our contentment, and allowing our happiness to be dependent upon forces and conditions outside of ourselves. TGINow!

"Accept what is, as it is, then do your best."
~ Maezumi Roshi

On the Mat: Notice how often your mind strays and takes you out of the moment, sabotaging you. Bring yourself back by refocusing on breath. Repeat the affirmation: "My serenity is directly proportionate to my acceptance of the moment" (Paula McFaden).

Awakening the Body: TGINow

- **Thunderbolt Pose** (Vajrasana), Stretches *Block*
- **Cat-Cow** (Marjaryasana)
- **Dolphin Pose**
- **Child's Pose** (Balasana)
- **Plank Pose**
- **Side Plank Pose** (Vasistasana)
- **Downward Facing Dog** (Adho Mukha Svanasana)
- **Standing Forward Fold** (Uttanasana)

Standing

- **Standing Stretches**
- **Cow Face Pose** (Gomukhasana) *Strap*
- **Half Sun Salutation** (Ardha Surya Namaskar)
- **Triangle Pose** (Trikonasana) *Block*
- **Reverse Triangle**
- **Intense Side Stretch Pose** (Parsvottanasana) *Blocks*
- **Revolved Triangle** (Parivrtta Trikonasana)
- **Standing Forward Fold** (Uttanasana)

Mat

- **Downward Facing Dog** (Adho Mukha Svanasana)
- **Child's Pose** (Balasana)
- **Boat Pose** (Navasana)
- **Marichi's Twist** (Marichyasana)
- **Supine Twists**
- **Corpse Pose** (Savasana)

*Repeat as a mantra: My serenity is directly proportionate
to my acceptance of the moment.*

Off the Mat: Throughout your day, be aware of your contentment in the moment as you connect with breath, then smile and say, "TGINow"!

Focus: Obstacles to Stillness

Many spiritual traditions strive for Enlightenment, or God-realization, which may be found through attaining stillness and quiet within.

> *"Be still and know that I am God" (Psalm 46:10)*
>
> *"Yoga is Stilling the fluctuations of the mind" (Yoga Sutra 1:2)*
>
> *"Equanimity of mind" (Krishna, Bhagavad Gita)*

What are the obstacles to attaining this peace of mind? If we want things to be different from the way they are in reality, we have the perception of dissatisfaction. Our fixed idea of how something *should* be sets us up for potential conflict, angst, and struggle. If anything shows up in our lives that happens to be out of line with our agenda, we get thrown off balance. We still need to do everything possible to create what we want, but without an expectation that it will turn out that way, without being attached to that result and dependent on it for our happiness.

> *"We must be willing to get rid of the life we've planned,*
> *so as to have the life that is waiting for us."*
> ~ Joseph Campbell

On the Mat: While practicing Witness Consciousness within a Four-Corner Awareness, we will strive to attain stillness and equanimity.

Awakening the Body: Stilling the mind
- **Child's Pose** (Balasana)
- **Extended Puppy Pose** (Uttana Shishosana)
- **Cat-Cow** (Marjaryasana)
- **Downward Facing Dog** (Adho Mukha Svanasana)
  - **Three-legged Dog**
  - **Fire Hydrant Pose**
- **Standing Forward Fold** (Uttanasana)
  - **Twist**
  - **Wrist Stretch** (Padahastasana)

Standing
- **Mountain Pose** (Tedasana)
- **Sun Salutation** (Surya Namaskar)
  - **Runner's Lunge**
  - **Low Lunge** (Anjaneyasana)
  - **Plank Pose**
  - **Cobra** (Bhujangasana)
  - **Plank Pose**
- **Standing Forward Fold** (Uttanasana)
- **Chair Pose** (Uttkatasana), Twist
- **Yoga Mudra** *Strap*

Mat
- **Seated Forward Fold** (Paschimottanasana)
- **Head to Knee Pose** (Janu Sirsasana), Twist
- **Supine Twists**
- **Corpse Pose** (Savasana)

*"Studying the Self through Witness Consciousness
allows you to be unbiased, clear, and objective...
Impersonal reality is the source of all solutions."*
~ Yogi Amrit Desai

Off the Mat: Throughout your day, see and feel yourself a part of
the whole of your surroundings, not just as one person, but of
all things within your awareness.

Focus: *Vairagya* — Detachment from Personal Desires

You have heard it said that unhappiness comes from wanting things to be different than the way they are right now. If your happiness and sense of peace is dependent upon external circumstances...when you lose weight, when you buy the new car, when you change jobs, etc....you are in the tenuous situation of constantly being bounced around by events often out of your control. Why put your happiness on hold? How would your sense of peace be if you didn't indulge in comparing yourself or your situation to others?

"Consider.
Wherever there is desire,
There is the world.

With resolute dispassion
Free yourself from desire,
And find happiness.

Desire binds you,
Nothing else.
Destroy it, and you are free.

Turn from the world.
Fulfill yourself,
And find lasting happiness."
~ Ashtavakra Gita, 10:3–4

On the Mat: Stay within your own experience within your poses, appreciating what is in this moment, without comparing yourself to others around you.

Awakening the Body: Within your own experience

- **Easy Seat** (Sukhasana), Stretches
- **Cat-Cow** (Marjaryasana), Twist
- **Dolphin Pose**
- **Plank Pose**
- **Child's Pose** (Balasana)
- **Downward Facing Dog** (Adho Mukha Svanasana)
- **Standing Forward Fold** (Uttanasana)

Standing

- **Half Sun Salutations** (Ardha Surya Namaskar)
- **Warrior II** (Virabhadrasana II)
- **Side Angle Pose** (Parsvottanasana) *Blocks* }
- **Triangle Pose** (Trikonasana) *Block* }
- **Reverse Triangle**
- **Eagle Pose** (Garudasana)
- **Standing Forward Fold** (Uttanasana)

Mat

- **Thunderbolt Pose** (Vajrasana), Twist
- **Bound Angle Pose** (Baddha Konasana)
- **Supine Twists**
- **Corpse Pose** (Savasana)

"The secret of happiness, you see, is not found in seeking more,
but in developing the capacity to enjoy less."

~ Dan Millman

Off the Mat: Throughout your day, be aware of and enjoy the positive aspects of each experience, and allow yourself to be happy right now, unconditionally.

Lesson Forty

𝒥ocus: **Awareness of the Beauty of the Moment**

"What do you like doing best in the world, Pooh?"

*"Well," said Pooh, "what I like best?" and then he had to
stop and think. Because although Eating Honey was a very
good thing to do, there was a moment just before you began
to eat it which was better than when you were, but he
didn't know what it was called."*
~ A.A. Milne, *House at Pooh Corner*

The honey doesn't taste quite as good, the goal doesn't mean quite as much, once the Destination is reached, but in that space just before Attainment, we are Aware and feel happy, if only for an instant, while enjoying the Journey. What if we could enjoy every bit of our time, both in those spaces beforehand, and then in the attainment of our dreams?

Pooh then says his favorite thing is being with Christopher Robin and Piglet, and "…it being a hummy sort of day outside, and birds singing." Ah, it's all in the awareness of the moment…

On the Mat: Be aware of enjoying each moment of your practice, regardless of reaching a goal or not, or even knowing what may come next.

Awakening the Body: Awareness of each moment
- On back, **Knees to Chest** (Apanasana)
- **Supine Twists**
- **Slow Bicycle Pumps**
- **Child's Pose** (Balasana)
- **Plank Pose**
- **Downward Facing Dog** (Adho Mukha Svanasana)
- **Standing Forward Fold** (Uttanasana)

Standing
- **Warrior I** (Virabhadrasana I)
- **Intense Side Stretch** (Parsvottanasana) *Blocks*
- **Revolved Triangle Pose** (Parivrtta Trikonasana)
- **Wide-legged Forward Fold** (Prasarita Padottanasana)
  - **Yoga Mudra**
- **Half Sun Salutation** (Ardha Surya Namaskar)

Mat
- **Easy Seat** (Sukhasana), Fold, Twist
- **Bridge Pose** (Setu Bandha Sarvangasana)
- **Supine Twists**
- **Corpse Pose** (Savasana)

"The clouds above us join and separate,
The breeze in the courtyard leaves and returns.
Life is like that, so why not relax?
Who can stop us from celebrating?"
~ Lu Yu, eighth-century Chinese poet

Off the Mat: You never know what the next minute will bring, so enjoy each moment as though time might stop and freeze you there.

Focus: Taking Responsibility for Ourselves

Many of our problems come from the mind within, rather than from external sources. To solve them, we need to stop blaming forces outside of ourselves, over which we have no control, and take an honest look at ourselves. Once we accept our responsibility in this, we will see that we have the key to happiness within us.

> *Once upon a time, there was a monk who had trouble meditating. Whenever he tried going into meditation, a giant spider would appear. No matter what he did, he could not get rid of it.*
>
> *At his wit's end, the monk sought help from his master. The master instructed him to prepare a brush at his side for the next attempt. When the spider appeared again, he was to use the brush to draw a circle on it.*
>
> *The monk followed these instructions and attempted meditation. Sure enough, the giant spider came back. The monk followed the plan and drew a circle on the monster. As soon as he did so, the spider disappeared, and he was able to resume meditation in peace.*
>
> *When he withdrew from the meditative state, the first thing he saw was a big black circle on his own belly. His worst enemy had been himself—exactly as the master had expected.*
>
> *~ The Monkey and the Spider Adapted from Derek Lin, The Tao of Daily Life*

On the Mat: Allow yourself to go within and ask: "Is there something that I want to change in my physical practice that is in my control, or do I have to just let it go?"

Awakening the Body: Restorative, for quiet within

- **Reclined Bound Angle** (Supta Badha Konasana) *Blankets, Blocks*
- **Legs up the Wall** (Viparita Karani) on *Block*
- **Cat-Cow** (Marjaryasana)
- **Extended Puppy Pose** (Uttana Shishosana)
- **Child's Pose** (Balasana)
- **Downward Facing Dog** (Adho Mukha Svanasana)
- **Standing Forward Fold** (Uttanasana) *Block*
  - **Big Toe Pose** (Padangusthasana)
  - **Wrist Stretch** (Padahastasana)

Standing

- **Sun Salutation** (Surya Namaskar)
  - **Runner's Lunge**
  - **Plank Pose**
  - **Downward Facing Dog** (Adho Mukha Svanasana)
- **Standing Forward Fold** (Uttanasana)

Mat

- **Noose Pose,** (Pasasana) heels on *Blanket*
- **Child's Pose** (Balasana)
- **Bridge Pose** (Setu Bandha Sarvangasana) *Block*
- **Supine Twists**
- **Corpse Pose** (Savasana), Extended

*"If there is a problem and there is nothing
you can do about it, there is no use worrying.*

*If there is something that can be done,
there is no use worrying.*

*And with that understanding can come
contentment and even joy."*

~ The Dalai Lama

Off the Mat: Look within for the …"serenity to accept the things you cannot change, the courage to change the things you can, and the wisdom to know the difference." (Serenity Prayer)

Lesson Forty-Two

𝒯ocus: Letting Go of Old Self-perceptions

How often does your belief that you *can't* stop you from even trying?

> *"The moments that take our breath away, and bring us to our knees also bring us closer to our greatness. For it is in those moments that we must choose…to remain small in the fear or stand tall in the knowing that **it is only when we let go of who we think we are that we can find who we can be.**"*
>
> ~ Dr. Dina Evan

On the 𝒨at: Don't allow your belief that you can't do a pose deter you from trying and seeing that you can indeed. Believe in yourself, and jump in.

Awakening the Body: Just do it

- **Thunderbolt Pose** (Vajrasana), Stretches
- **Child's Pose** (Balasana)
- **Plank Pose**
- **Side Plank Pose** (Vasisthasana)
- **Child's Pose** (Balasana)
- **Downward Facing Dog** (Adho Mukho Svanasana), Twist
- **Standing Forward Fold** (Uttanasana), Twist

Standing

- **Standing Stretches**
- **Warrior II** (Virabhadrasana II)
- **Reverse Warrior**
- **Wide-legged Forward Fold** (Prasarita Padottanasana)
- **Chair Pose** (Uttkatasana), Twist
- **Yoga Mudra**

Mat

- **Cat-Cow** (Marjaryasana)
- **Cow Face Pose** (Gomukhasana) *Strap*
- **Seated Forward Fold** (Paschimottanasana)
- **Supine Twists**
- **Corpse Pose** (Savasana)

"Man ponders his fate day and night,
And by doing so creates his own
Destiny while sitting in contemplation,
Wasting precious time."

~ Sandi Greenberg

Off the Mat: Make a list of things in your life that you have been hesitant to attempt and form a personal intention to "just do it," one by one.

*F*ocus: **Letting Go of Old Beliefs**

Letting go, or non-attachment, is encouraged in yoga, which would apply to material possessions, unhealthy relationships, old clothes, old self-perceptions and outdated thinking. It is about freeing oneself from pain-producing beliefs, fears, and desires.

We let go of the old to make way for the new, including old pro-gramming of our beliefs about ourselves from previous life periods and life situations that no longer apply to who we are today. What story defined us then, and which one do we want to define us now?

Just as we take our old clothes to second-hand stores, we can begin shedding our old ideas and begin to trust in our own truth and in our present-day perceptions.

*"We each move forward secure on our own
earth, not the earth of others.*

*Happiness is something we must create for
ourselves. No one else can give it to us."*

~ Daisaku Ikeda

On the *M*at: Consciously let go of tension while in each pose, as well as the pre-programmed beliefs that are keeping you from the full expression of all you can do.

Awakening the Body: Letting go
- **Child's Pose** (Balasana)
- **Cat-Cow** (Marjaryasana)
- **Gate Pose** (Parighasana) *Block*
- **Downward Facing Dog** (Adho Mukho Svanasana)
- **Standing Forward Fold** (Uttanasana)

Standing
- **Upward Salute** (Ardhva Hastasana)
- **Triangle Pose** (Trikonasana) *Block* ⎫
- **Reverse Triangle** ⎬
- **Eagle Pose** (Garudasana) ⎭
- **Standing Forward Fold** (Uttanasana)
  - ○ **Twist**
- **Sun Salutation** (Surya Namaskar)
  - ○ **Plank Pose**
  - ○ **Cobra** (Bhujangasana), variations
  - ○ **Downward Facing Dog** (Adho Mukha Svanasana)

Mat
- **Child's Pose** (Balasana)
- **Head to Knee Pose** (Janu Sirsasana)
- **Supine Twists**
- **Corpse Pose** (Savasana)

"Self-trust is the first secret of success."
~ Ralph Waldo Emerson

Off the Mat: Set an intention to consciously let go of one pre-programmed belief that you feel is keeping you stuck in life, and throughout your week ask yourself, "How is this working for me?" When you're ready, add another.

Lesson Forty-Four

Focus: **Beware of Blind Belief**

There are many dangers inherent in blindly believing something to be true without first experiencing it yourself and knowing that truth, or lack of it. The key to knowing the truth of anything is to focus on your own experience with it, to go out and do the work yourself. By being mindful and aware, you can ask yourself how each situation is serving you, then trust in your intuition.

"If you experience it, it's the truth.
The same thing believed is a lie."

~ Werner Erhard

On the Mat: Do you feel secure in your poses, and connected to the energy of the earth? Do you feel secure in your own truth?

Awakening the Body: Feeling grounded and secure
- **Reclined Bound Angle Pose** (Supta Baddha Konasana)
- **Reclined Big Toe Pose** (Supta Padangusthasana) *Strap*
- **Bound Angle Pose** (Baddha Konasana), Fold
- **Child's Pose** (Balasana)
- **Downward Facing Dog** (Adho Mukha Svanasana)
- **Standing Forward Fold** (Uttanasana)

Standing
- **Mountain Pose** (Tedasana)
- **Tree Pose** (Vrksasana)
- **Chair Pose** (Uttkatasana), Twist
- **Sun Salutation** (Surya Namaskar)
  - **Low Lunge** (Anjaneyasana)
  - **Runner's Lunge**
  - **Intense Side Stretch** (Parsvottanasana)
  - **Downward Facing Dog** (Adho Mukha Svanasana)

Mat
- **Camel Pose** (Ustrasana) *Blocks*
- **Child's Pose** (Balasana)
- **Seated Forward Fold** (Paschimottanasana)
- **Bridge Pose** (Setu Bandha Sarvangasana) *Block*
- **Supine Twists**
- **Corpse Pose** (Savasana)

> *"Believe nothing, no matter where you read it or who
> has said it, not even if I have said it, unless it agrees with
> your own reason and your own common sense."*
> ~ The Buddha

Off the Mat: Set an intention to test your own truth in each situation. Ask, "How is this serving me?", then trust your heart and gut feeling.

ℱocus: **Yoga is in Everything**

With awareness you can see that the opportunity for practicing yoga is in nearly everything you do and everywhere you go.

> *"Yoga is in everything I do as I move through my day — as I journal in the morning, as I drive my car, as I'm teaching, as I'm washing the dishes. There's yoga in how I interact with people, as well as how I treat myself. It's about being mindful, connecting with my breath, releasing stress, and being in tune with the spirit of life."*
>
> ~ Abigail Jefferson

On the Mat: As you move through the poses, practice *Ahimsa* (non-harming) by respecting your body and not judging yourself, and *Satya* (truth) by respecting your limitations. Deal with the reality of what is arising, not what you think should be happening. Connect to your breath to keep yourself in the moment. You see, it's all yoga…body, mind, and spirit.

Awakening the Body: Responding as a Yogi

- **Easy Seat** (Sukhasana)
  - **Kapalabhati** (Skull Brightening) **Breath**
  - **Side Stretches**
- **Cat-Cow** (Marjaryasana), Twists
- **Child's Pose** (Balasana)
- **Side Plank Pose** (Vasisthasana)
- **Downward Facing Dog** (Adho Mukha Svanasana), Twist
- **Standing Forward Fold** (Uttanasana)

Standing

- **Standing Stretches**
- **Eagle Pose** (Garudasana)
- **Warrior II** (Virabhadrasana II)
- **Reverse Warrior**
- **Side Angle Pose** (Parsvakonasana)
- **Yoga Mudra**
- **Standing Forward Fold** (Uttanasana), Twist

Mat

- **Head to Knee Pose** (Janu Sirsasana)
- **Half Lord of the Fishes Pose** (Ardha Matyendrasana)
- **Supine Twists**
- **Corpse Pose** (Savasana)

"Yoga is an art as well as a science. It is a science, because it offers practical methods for controlling body and mind, thereby making deep meditation possible. And it is an art, for unless it is practiced intuitively and sensitively it will yield only superficial results."
~ Paramahansa Yogananda

Off the Mat: Notice the yoga in your day: how you react in traffic, while waiting in line at the store, performing a tedious task, when someone cancels an appointment at the last minute, when receiving disappointing news, or when someone doesn't behave as you would like. Yoga informs your relationship to others and your attitude toward yourself. Yoga is in everything you do.

ℱocus: **Choose to Live a Life that Matters**

"Ready or not, someday it will all come to an end. There will be no more sunrises, no minutes, hours or days. All the things you collected, whether treasured or forgotten, will pass to someone else. Your wealth, fame and temporal power will shrivel to irrelevance. It will not matter what you owned or what you were owed. Your grudges, resentments, frustrations, and jealousies will finally disappear.

So, too, your hopes, ambitions, plans, and to-do lists will expire. The wins and losses that once seemed so important will fade away. It won't matter where you came from, or on what side of the tracks you lived, at the end. It won't matter whether you were beautiful or brilliant. Even your gender and skin color will be irrelevant.

So what will matter? How will the value of your days be measured? What will matter is not what you bought, but what you built; not what you got, but what you gave. What will matter is not your success, but your significance. What will matter is not what you learned, but what you taught. What will matter is every act of integrity, compassion, courage or sacrifice that enriched, empowered or encouraged others to emulate your example.

What will matter is not your competence, but your character. What will matter is not how many people you knew, but how many will feel a lasting loss when you're gone. What will matter are not your memories, but the memories that live in those who loved you. What will matter is how long you will be remembered, by whom and for what. Living a life that matters doesn't happen by accident. It's not a matter of circumstance, but of choice. Choose to live a life that matters."

~ Author unknown

On the Mat: Don't judge your performance in a pose as good or bad, but rather laud and appreciate yourself for just being here and doing this for yourself. Also acknowledge how this benefits others.

Awakening the Body: Choose awareness
- **Easy Seat** (Sukhasana)
  - **Three-Part Breathing**
  - **Stretches**
  - **Eagle Pose** (Garudasana), arms
- **Cat-Cow** (Marjaryasana)
- **Gate Pose** (Parighasana) *Block*
- **Child's Pose** (Balasana)
- **Downward Facing Dog** (Adho Mukha Svanasana)
- **Standing Forward Fold** (Uttanasana)

Standing
- **Warrior II** (Virabhadrasana II)
- **Reverse Warrior**
- **Side Angle Pose** (Parsvakonasana)
- **Runner's Lunge**
- **Plank Pose**
- **Locust Pose** (Salambhasana)
- **Downward Facing Dog** (Adho Mukha Svanasana)

Mat
- **Child's Pose** (Balasana)
- **Thunderbolt Pose** (Vajrasana), Twist, Back Bend
- **Supine Twists**
- **Corpse Pose** (Savasana)

"Living a life that matters doesn't happen by accident. It's not a matter of circumstance, but of choice. Choose to live a life that matters."

Off the Mat: Think of just one thing that you can do today to improve someone's life or to bring a smile to someone's face, even if for the moment.

Focus: **Life is Circular** — Give of Yourself Fully

Life is circular, so by giving, you receive, both materially and spiritually.

If people stop spending money, the economy would be in turmoil. Without shoppers, stores close, so people lose their jobs and security. They then can't partake of your services and products, so you suffer, can't shop, and lose your security. Therefore, by putting your money into circulation, you eventually profit, and by giving to others, you feel the spiritual benefit as well. Give until it feels good.

This is especially true of giving love, time, and energy to others. By giving of yourself and not holding back, you are fulfilled and rewarded. Visualize a bowl of food. As the food is passed out amongst the hungry, the bowl keeps refilling, keeps replenishing itself. Likewise, the more you give of yourself, the more you get back.

"When you give yourself, you receive more than you give."
~ Antoine de Saint-Exupery

On the Mat: Set an intention for full presence with full energy in every pose. Feel your heart open, uplift, and fill. Feel the energy flowing through and around you, from the tips of your fingers to the tips of your toes.

Awakening the Body: Full presence, full energy
- **Half Sun Salutation** (Ardha Surya Namaskar)
- **Yoga Mudra**
- **Standing Forward Fold** (Uttanasana)
  - Twist
  - **Big Toe Pose** (Padangusthasana)
- **Half Sun Salutation** (Ardha Surya Namaskar)

Standing
- **Triangle Pose** (Trikonasana)
- **Revolved Triangle**
- **Sun Salutation** (Surya Namaskar)
  - **Runner's Lunge**
  - **Low Lunge** (Anjaneyasana), Twist
  - **Plank Pose**
  - **Downward Facing Dog** (Adho Mukha Svanasana) }

Mat
- **Child's Pose** (Balasana)
- **Head to Knee Pose** (Janu Sirsasana)
- **Half Lord of Fishes Pose** (Ardha Matsyendrasana)
- **Supine Twists**
- **Corpse Pose** (Savasana)

*"The best way to find yourself is to
lose yourself in the service of others."*
~ Mohandas Gandhi

Off the Mat: How can you be fully in the moment and give until it feels good today?

Lesson Forty-Eight

𝒥ocus: Finding Balance for Peace of Mind

Knowing when and how to create balance in a situation is difficult, unless one is always in a state of equilibrium, which is not usually the case. Realizing that there is no hill without a valley, no up without a down, helps us accept any situation as it is, without wishing it were otherwise, which is the cause of all unhappiness.

*"We must learn to be still in the midst of activity
and to be vibrantly alive in repose."*
~ Indira Gandhi

On the 𝒨at: Notice the equal and opposite movements in the poses that create a feeling of balance in the body. Set an intention to find that "sweet spot" in each pose.

Awakening the Body: Feel the balance

- On back, feel the body on the earth
- **Legs up the Wall** (Viparita Karani) on *Block* or wall
- **Child's Pose** (Balasana)
- **Downward Facing Dog** (Adho Mukha Svanasana)
- **Standing Forward Fold** (Uttanasana)

Standing

- **Upward Salute** (Urdhva Hastasana), Stretches
- **Warrior I** (Virabhadrasana I)
- **Intense Side Stretch Pose** (Parsvottanasana)
- **Plank Pose**
- **Downward Facing Dog** (Adho Mukha Svanasana)
- **Standing Forward Fold** (Uttanasana)
- **Yoga Mudra**

Mat

- **Child's Pose** (Balasana)
- **Seated Forward Fold** (Paschimottanasana)
- **Bridge Pose** (Setu Bandha Sarvangasana)
- **Reclined Bound Angle** (Supta Baddha Konasana), Lifted
- **Supine Twists**
- **Corpse Pose** (Savasana)

"Perfection in an asana is achieved when the effort to perform it becomes effortless and the infinite being within is reached."
~ B.K.S. Iyengar

Off the Mat: Look for that "sweet spot" in your activities during the day, that place of balance and equilibrium that allows you to accept and be mindful of what is, that perfection that is achieved when effort is released and you are quiet within.

𝓕ocus: Spring Cleaning for Body and Mind

Spring is a beautiful season of renewal, though thoughts of spring cleaning bring groans as well as pleasure, as we think of letting go of the old and welcoming the new. This is true of giving away or selling old clothes that no longer fit or suit us, shedding old relationships that no longer work for us, as well as old programming of our beliefs about ourselves from previous life periods and situations that no longer apply to who we are today.

We can spring clean our bodies and minds as well using *Pranayama* (breathing) techniques and *Asana* twists to cleanse and detoxify our internal organs. More peace and space in the body brings more peace and space in the mind.

> *"To care for the body is a duty, otherwise*
> *the mind will not be strong and clear."*
> ~ The Buddha

On the 𝓜at: Picture each targeted part of the body as you send your healing energy to it. Fully inhale the fresh, purifying air and fully exhale the old, toxic air.

Awakening the Body: Refresh and renew

Seated in Chair:
- **Alternate-Nostril Breathing** (Nadi Sodhana)
- **Forward Fold** (Uttanasana)
- **Side Stretches**
- **Bharadvaja's Twist** (Bharadvajasana)
- **Forward Fold** (Uttanasana)

Standing with Chair:
- **Downward Facing Dog** (Adho Mukha Svanasana)
  - **Three-legged Dog**
- **Revolved Triangle** (Parivrtta Trikonasana)
- **Chair Pose** (Uttkatasana), Twist

Mat
- **Restorative Forward Twist** *Blankets*
- **Staff Pose** (Dandasana)
- **Half Lord of Fishes Pose** (Ardha Matsyendrasana)
- **Bound Angle Pose** (Baddha Konasana)
- **Supine Stretches**
- **Corpse Pose** (Savasana), Standard, or legs up on chair

"Without purity in body and mind, clarity eludes us. The immensity and luminosity of our true selves and our connection to spirit and to each other becomes clouded. The transparency we cultivate in Saucha [Purity] enables us to reflect the divine more completely in all our relationships."
~ Swami Shraddhananda

Off the Mat: Be mindful of what you eat, drink, say, and hear, asking yourself: "How does this serve the purity of my body, mind, and spirit?"

Lesson Fifty

$\mathcal{F}$ocus: Everything is Impermanent

A very poignant expression of the impermanence of life is exemplified by the Tibetan monks, who spend weeks or months making an intricately designed sand mandala, grain by grain, which once completed, is destroyed in celebration.

So many of us are agitated and frustrated by the fact that we can no longer practice certain poses, both on the mat and in life, because of advancing age or illness, and we mourn the loss of youth and health. Suffering is caused within us from remaining attached to the practices of our past, to not accepting and living in this moment with what is.

We cannot control the impermanence of life, but we can recognize that our suffering is based on our reaction to that impermanence, over which we do have some control.

"Life? Butterfly on a swaying grass,
That's all.
But exquisite."

~ Nishiyama Soin

On the $\mathcal{M}$at: Notice your reaction to any frustration you may face in a pose and seek to find the true source of it.

Awakening the Body: Accepting the present reality

- **Reclined Bound Angle** (Supta Baddha Konasana) *Blankets, Blocks*
- **Reclined Big Toe Pose** (Supta Padangustasana) *Strap*
- **Extended Puppy Pose** (Uttana Shishosana)
- **Child's Pose** (Balasana)
- **Downward Facing Dog** (Adho Mukha Svanasana)
- **Standing Forward Fold** (Uttanasana)

Standing

- **Warrior II** (Virabhadrasana II) }
- **Side Angle Pose** (Parsvakonasana) }
- **Sun Salutation** (Surya Namaskar)
  - **Low Lunge** (Anjaneyasana)
  - **Plank Pose**
  - **Cobra Pose** (Bhujangasana)
  - **Plank Pose**
  - **Pigeon Pose** (Eka Pada Rajakapotasana)
  - **Downward Facing Dog** (Adho Mukha Svanasana)
- **Standing Forward Fold** (Uttanasana)

Mat

- **Child's Pose** (Balasana)
- **Head to Knee Pose** (Janu Sirsasana)
- **Bound Angle Pose** (Baddha Konasana), Fold, Twist
- **Supine Twists**
- **Corpse Pose** (Savasana)

"Impermanence is the nature of the human condition"
~ The Buddha

Off the Mat: During the day, notice your reactions when things aren't as you would like them to be and once again ask yourself the source of those reactions. Notice how this awareness serves you.

Lesson Fifty-One

Focus: Forgiveness — The Importance of Letting Go

Yoga encourages us to let go...Let go of attachments to possessions, to the results of our actions, to harmful habits and relationships, to greed. We also are encouraged to let go of anger and resentments, toward others and ourselves, as major elements that disturb our ultimate goal of finding peace of mind and happiness now. An unknown author wrote that "to forgive is to set a prisoner free and discover that the prisoner was you."

> *"As long as we are unable to forgive, we keep ourselves chained to the unforgiven. We give them rent-free space in our minds, emotional shackles on our hearts, and the right to torment us in the small hours of the night."*
> ~ Diana Robinson

On the Mat: Practice letting go mentally, of expectations of how you should appear in each pose, and physically, of tension and holding within the body.

Awakening the Body: Release and relax
- **Restorative Forward Twist** *Blankets*
- **Child's Pose** (Balasana)
- **Dolphin Pose**
- **Child's Pose** (Balasana)
- **Downward Facing Dog** (Adho Mukha Svanasana)
- **Standing Forward Fold** (Uttanasana)

Standing
- **Half Sun Salutations** (Ardha Surya Namaskar)
- **Triangle Pose** (Trikonasana)
- **Reverse Triangle**
- **Wide-legged Forward Fold** (Prasarita Padottanasana)
  - o **Yoga Mudra** (First Side)
  - o Twist (Second Side)
- **Standing Stretches**

Mat
- **Thread the Needle**
- **Child's Pose** (Balasana)
- **Easy Seat** (Sukhasana), Twist, Fold
- **Reclined Big Toe Pose** (Supta Hasta Padangustasana) *Strap*
- **Supine Twists**
- **Corpse Pose** (Savasana)

"Go not to the temple to ask for forgiveness for your sins,
but first forgive those who have sinned against you."
~ Rabindranath Tagore, poet

Off the Mat: Practice letting go of old angers and resentments as they arise in your mind by connecting to breath, and enjoy the peace of mind that follows once you've set them, and yourself, free.

Focus: Life is a Mystery

When we feel we are in the throes of misfortune and unhappiness, we hate to hear someone say, "Things happen for the best," however, there are occasions in our lives which seem like great misfortunes at the time but have turned out to be blessings in disguise. Of course, the reverse can also be true.

"This being human is a guest house,
Every morning a new arrival.
A joy, a depression, a meanness
Some momentary awareness comes as an unexpected visitor.

Welcome and entertain them all!
Even if they're a crowd of sorrows
Who violently sweep your house empty of its furniture.
Still, treat each guest honorably.
He may be clearing you out for some new delight."
~ Rumi, The Guest House

Life is indeed a wonderful mystery, and we don't know what will happen from one day to the next or why it is happening at all. If we refrain from making judgments and labeling events as good or bad, we can make space for what Is in every moment, and "welcome and entertain them all."

On the Mat: Notice your reaction to how you are showing up in your poses today. Try not to have expectations, refrain from judging yourself, and simply be open to what is. Then be aware of how this serves your inner sense of peace.

Awakening the Body: Every time a first time
- **Bound Angle** (Baddha Konasana), Stretches, Fold
- **Child's Pose** (Balasana)
- **Gate Pose** (Parighasana) *Block*
- **Side Plank Pose** (Vasisthasana)
- **Child's Pose** (Balasana)
- **Cat-Cow** (Marjaryasana)
- **Downward Facing Dog** (Adho Mukha Svanasana)
- **Standing Forward Fold** (Uttanasana)

Standing
- **Mountain Pose** (Tedasana)
- **Eagle Pose** (Garudasana)
- **Yoga Mudra**
- **Sun Salutation** (Surya Namaskar)
  - **Plank Pose**
  - **Pigeon Pose** (Eka Pada Rajakapotasana) *Blanket* ⎫
  - **Downward Facing Dog** (Adho Mukha Svanasana) ⎭

Mat
- **Child's Pose** (Balasana)
- **Happy Baby** (Ananda Balasana)
- **Figure Four Stretch**
- **Supine Twists**
- **Corpse Pose** (Savasana)

"Nirvana is.
You are.
Let yourself experience this truth."
~ Scott Shaw

Off the Mat: Stepping into Witness Consciousness, observe your daily events and your responses to them. Be open to whatever arises, without labeling, and be aware of how this serves your inner sense of peace.

References

All quotes used in this book have been documented whenever possible. Often, however, a quote is found and loved, put away for future enjoyment, and though the author is cited, the source is not known or accessible.

Introduction

Sogyal Rinpoche, The Tibetan Book of Living and Dying, in *Contemplative Living*, by Joan Duncan Oliver, pg. 139

Consciousness, by Nomi Sharron, author of, soon-to-be-published, *Tony Samara: The Making of a Modern Shaman... and Beyond.*

Lesson

1. Rumi, in *Light Upon Light*, Andrew Harvey, pg. 104

2. Yogi Amrit Desai, *Amrit Yoga and the Yoga Sutras*, pg. 65
    The Talmud, Pirkei Avot, 4:1

3. Nischala Joy Devi, *The Secret Power of Yoga*, pg. 193
    The Living Gita, VI:16, commentary by Sri Swami Satchidananda

4. *The Living Gita*, V:11–12, commentary by Sri Swami Satchidananda
    William Shakespeare, *Hamlet, The Player King*

5. Yogi Amrit Desai, *Amrit Yoga and the Yoga Sutras*, pg. 69
    Yogi Amrit Desai, *Amrit Yoga and the Yoga Sutras*, pg. 70

6. Nischala Joy Devi, *The Secret Power of Yoga*, pg. 205
    Patanjali, *The Yoga Sutras*, II:2, translated by Sri Swami Satchidananda

7. Judith Lasater, quoted in *Holistic Health* online magazine, "Tapas (Burning Zeal)—Step #8-Steps on the Path", by Judi England, March 8, 2009, *http://blog.timesunion.com/holistichealth/tapas-burning-zeal-step-8-on-the-path/906*
All Spirit Fitness, online magazine, *http://www.allspiritfitness.com/library/features/aa102604a.shtml*

8. Thich Nhat Hanh, *Peace is Every Step*, pg. 38

9. B.K.S. Iyengar, *Light on the Yoga Sutras*, Thorsons, 1993
Lama Surya Das, *http://www.soulfulliving.com/let_go_surya_das.htm*

10. Eric Walrabenstein (Yogi E), verbal communication
Swami Kripalvananda, unknown source

11. Swami Karunanand in "Prescriptions for Pranayama", on-line Yoga Journal by Claudia Cummins, *http://www.yogajournal.com/practice/673*
Hatha Yoga Pradipika, Ch. 11.2

12. Sri Swami Satchidananda, in *The Yoga Sutras of Patanjali*, pg. 166

13. Patanjali, *Yoga Sutras*, 11:2
Hans Margolius, unknown source

14. Bhante Henepola Gunaratana (Sri Lankan Buddhist monk)
Judith Lasater, *Yoga Journal, http://www.yogajournal.com/wisdom/461*, "Seeking Samadhi"

15. The Buddha, unknown source
Nischala Joy Devi, *The Secret Power of Yoga*, pg. 25

16. Thich Nhat Hanh, *Peace is Every Step*, pg. 38

17. Eric Walrabenstein (Yogi E), verbal communication

18. Phillip Moffitt, "Selfless Gratitude," *Yoga Journal*, August, 2002
Paul, 1 Thessalonians 5:18

19. Ram Dass, unknown source

20. Sri Swami Satchidananda, *The Yoga Sutras of Patanjali*, pg. 91
    Carl Jung, Swiss psychologist (1875–1961)

21. Patanjali, *The Yoga Sutras*, II:2
    TKV Desikachar, *The Heart of Yoga*

22. Thich Nhat Hanh, *The Heart of the Buddha's Teaching*, pg. 196
    Deepak Chopra, unknown source

23. Deepak Chopra, *The Seven Spiritual Laws of Success*, pg. 81
    T.S Eliott, *The Four Quartets*, "East Coker," V)

24. Cherokee Indian legend
    Thomas Merton, unknown source

25. Jane Gleason, verbal communication
    Jon Kabat-Zinn, *Wherever You Go There You Are: Mindfulness
        Meditation in Everyday Life*, 1994 (Hyperion, N.Y.)

26. The Buddha, unknown source

27. *The Theragatha, Verses of the Elder Monks*, a Buddist
        scripture and collection of short poems supposedly recited
        by early members of the Buddhist sangha
    The Living Gita, V1:17, commentary by Sri Swami
        Satchidananda

28. The Buddha, unknown source

29. Sally Kempton, "Me Talk Pretty", *Yoga Journal*, Aug. 18, 2006

30. Wu Men, Buddhist monk and poet, unknown source
    Mother Teresa, unknown source

31. Lao Tsu, *Hua Hu Ching*
    Deepak Chopra, *The Seven Spiritual Laws of Yoga*, pg. 19

32. Thich Nhat Hanh, *Being Peace*

33. Lao Tsu, *Tao Te Ching*, V
    Ram Dass, unknown source

34. Adapted from Derek Lin, *The Tao of Daily Life*, pg. 111
    Oprah Winfrey on-line magazine

35. Adapted from Derek Lin, *The Tao of Daily Life*, pg. 108
    Peggy Jenkins, *To Discover Joy*, pg. 3–4

36. Eckhardt Tolle, *The Power of Now*, pg. 11
    Norman Vincent Peale, unknown source

37. Maezumi Roshi, unknown source
    Paula McFaden, verbal communication

38. Joseph Campbell, unknown source
    Yogi Amrit Desai, unknown source

39. *Ashtavakra Gita*, 10:3–4
    Dan Millman, *The Way of the Peaceful Warrior*, pg. 162

40. A.A. Milne, *The House on Pooh Corner*, pg. 168
    Lu Yu, 8th-century Chinese poet, unknown source

41. Adapted from Derek Lin, *The Tao of Daily Life*, pg. 31
    The Dalai Lama, unknown source

42. Dr. Dina Evan, Life Coach, Phoenix, Arizona
    Sandi Greenberg

43. Daisaku Ikeda, President, Soka Gakkai International
    Ralph Waldo Emerson, unknown source

44. Werner Erhard, unknown source
    The Buddha, unknown source

45. Abigail Jefferson, in *Yoga Journal*, May, 2009
    Paramhansa Yogananda, unknown source

46. Author unknown

47. Antoine de Saint-Exupery, unknown source
    Mohandas Gandhi, unknown source

48. Indira Gandhi, unknown source
    B.K.S. Iyengar, translator, *Patanjali's Yoga Sutras*, II:47

49. The Buddha, unknown source
    Swami Shraddhananda, unknown source

50. Nishiyama Soin, unknown source
    The Buddha, unknown source

51. Diana Robinson, "The Top Ten Steps of Forgiveness"
    Rabindranath Tagore, poet, unknown source

52. Rumi, *The Essential Rumi*, pg. 109
    Scott Shaw, *Nirvana in a Nutshell*, pg. 3

Pose
Glossary

Big Toe Pose *(Padangusthasana)*

Boat Pose *(Navasana)*

Bound Angle Pose *(Baddha Konasana)*

Bridge Pose *(Setu Bandha Sarvangasana)*

Camel Pose *(Ustrasana)*

Cat-Cow I *(Marjaryasana)*

Cat-Cow II *(Marjaryasana)*

Chair Pose *(Uttkatasana)*

Chair Twist *(Bharadvajasana)*

Child's Pose *(Balasana)*

Cobra Pose *(Bhujangasana)*

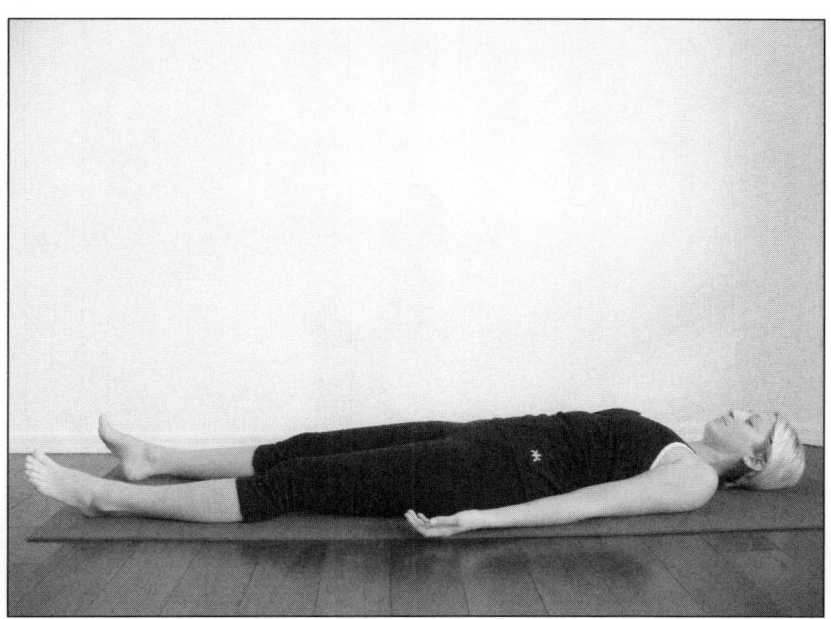

Corpse Pose *(Savasana)*

Cow Face Pose *(Gomukhasana)*

Cresent Pose

Dolphin Pose

Downward Facing Dog *(Adho Mukha Svanasana)*

Eagle Pose *(Garudasana)*

Easy Seat *(Sukhasana)*

Extended Puppy Pose *(Uttana Shishosana)*

Figure Four Stretch

Fire Hydrant Pose

Garland Pose *(Malasana)*

Half Lord of Fishes *(Ardha Matsyendrasana)*

Happy Baby *(Ananda Balasana)*

Head to Knee Forward Fold *(Janu Sirsasana)*

Intense Side Stretch *(Parsvottanasana)*

Legs up the Wall *(Viparita Karani)*

Lion's Pose *(Simhasana)*

Low Lunge *(Anjaneyasana)*

Marichi's Twist *(Marichyasana)*

Mountain Pose *(Tedasana)*

Noose Pose *(Pasasana)*

Pigeon Pose I *(Eka Pada Rajakapotasana)*

Pigeon Pose II *(Eka Pada Rajakapotasana)*

Plank Pose

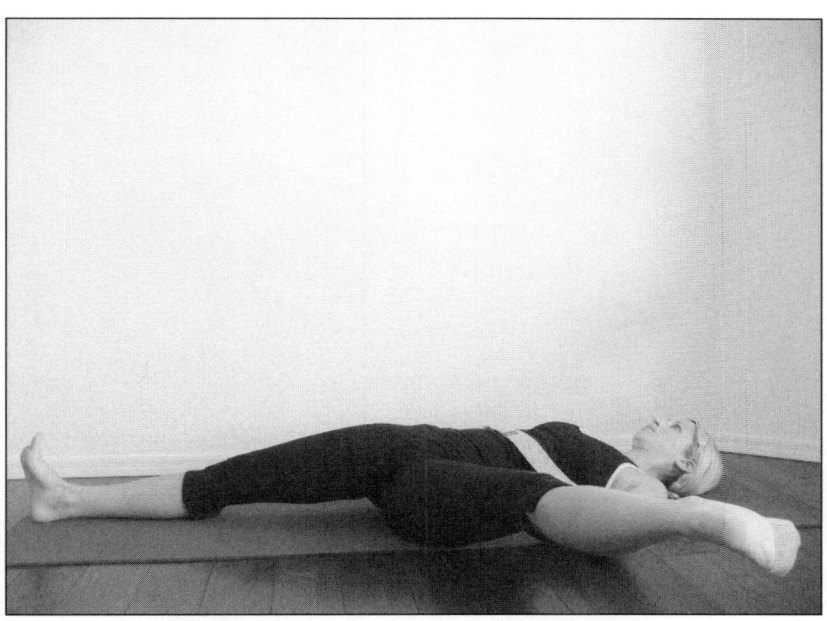

Reclining Big Toe Pose *(Supta Padangusthasana)*

Reclining Bound Angle *(Supta Baddha Konasana)*

Restorative Forward Fold

Reverse Triangle

Reverse Warrior

Runner's Lunge

Seated Forward Fold *(Paschimottanasana)*

Side Angle Pose *(Parsvakonasana)*

Side Plank Pose I *(Vasistasana)*

Side Plank Pose II *(Vasistasana)*

Staff Pose *(Dondasana)*

Standing Forward Fold *(Uttanasana)*

Sun Salutation *(Surya Namaskar)* A

Sun Salutation *(Surya Namaskar)* B

Sun Salutation *(Surya Namaskar)* C

Sun Salutation *(Surya Namaskar)* D

Sun Salutation *(Surya Namaskar)* E

Sun Salutation *(Surya Namaskar)* F

Sun Salutation *(Surya Namaskar)* G

Sun Salutation *(Surya Namaskar)* H

Sun Salutation *(Surya Namaskar)* I

Supine Twist I

Supine Twist II

Thread the Needle

Three-legged Dog

Thunderbolt Pose *(Vajrasana)*

Tree Pose *(Vrksasana)*

Triangle Pose *(Trikonasana)*

Upward Plank Pose *(Purvottanasana)*

Upward Salute *(Urdhva Hastasana)*

Warrior I *(Virabhadrasana I)*

Warrior II *(Virabhadrasana II)*

Warrior III *(Virabhadrasana III)*

Wide Legged Forward Fold *(Upavistha Konasana)*

Yoga Mudra

Glossary of Terms

Pranayama: A Sanskrit word meaning "restraint of the *prana* or life force" and is the fourth of Patanjali's Eight Limbs of yoga. It is practiced to control, harmonize, and synchronize the breath with and for the asana and meditative practices. (Guidance by a teacher in order to first learn the correct procedure is advised.) Some forms of Pranayama are as follows:

Equal Breath *(Sama Vritti):* The inhalation and exhalation are of the same, equal, length. For instance, a slow count of four upon inhalation, then a pause of retention, is followed by a slow count of four on the exhalation, with a pause. The number counted is not prescribed, but depends upon the individual.

Three-Part Breath (Yogic Breath): Basic to both meditation and asana practices, this involves a slow, deep inhalation through the nostrils, filling up the abdomen, the diaphragm, then the heart space, up to the collarbones with air. The slow exhalation is in the reverse order.

Skull-Brightening Breath *(Kapalabhati):* Inhale deeply through both nostrils, expanding the abdomen, and exhale with a forceful contraction of abdominal muscles. Pull the abdomen in by quickly contracting the abdominal muscles and exhale through the nose. The air is pushed out of the lungs by the natural contraction of the diaphragm.

Alternate-Nostril Breath (*Nadi Sodhana*): As the name infers, the breathing is done alternating between the two nostrils. Sit in a comfortable asana while bending the right elbow and hold the hand up in *Mrigi Mudra,* with the pointer and middle fingers bent onto the palm and the ring finger resting on the little finger.

With eyes closed, close the right nostril with your right thumb and inhale through the left nostril. Do this to the count of four seconds.

Immediately close the left nostril with your right ring finger and little finger, and at the same time remove your thumb from the right nostril, and exhale through this nostril to the count of four seconds.

Inhale through the right nostril to the count of four seconds. Close the right nostril with your right thumb and exhale through the left nostril to the count of four seconds. This completes one full round.

Ujjai (Victorious) **Breath**: This is used to generate heat and as a point of focus for the mind in order to stay present. The inhalation and exhalation are both done through the nose, with the "ocean" or "Darth Vader" sound created by narrowing the throat passage.

Bare Attention: A meditative technique that allows for an awareness of everything around you non-selectively and non-judgmentally. It is an un-focusing, an inclusion, of all sensations and objects in your awareness into the whole picture, which includes your thoughts, all holding the same weight and importance.

Four-Corner Awareness: All four corners of the room in which you are practicing are in your mind's eye, as well as all things within the room, simultaneously and inclusively, within your awareness. You and your thoughts become part of the whole picture.

Witness Consciousness: That part of your mind which is able to observe thoughts as they arise, without reacting, judging, or labeling, while maintaining the attitude of a detached, but kind observer. A traditional metaphor for this energy of mindfulness is that it is similar to the deepest part of an ocean, which remains calm and silent even if waves (of emotion or sensation) are raging at its surface.

In loving memory of my brother,

David Allen Chez

If I only knew then what I know now...

Journal
Pages

Journal

Journal

Journal

Journal

Journal

Journal

Journal

Journal

Journal

Journal

Journal

Journal

Journal

Journal

Journal

Journal

Journal

About the Author

Sandi Greenberg has her 500-hour certification training as a yoga teacher, her Bachelor and Master's Degrees in Literature, as well as certifications as a life coach and hypnotherapist. She has been an educator, counselor, and mentor for several decades in the academic and fitness fields, both in Israel and in the United States. Her mission is to help people attain peace of mind, clarity, direction, and empowerment and help them maximize their physical health and well being by sharing the tools and talents that have benefited her over the years. Sandi lives in Phoenix, Arizona with her husband Mark, where she teaches yoga, writes, and coaches.

Visit Sandi Greenberg online at *www.NoPlaceLikeOmYoga.com* to inquire about the book or classes and coaching services.

⟡ Direct Order Form ⟡

Your Yoga Experience:
52 Comprehensive Lessons for Lifelong Practice

Available online at *www.NoPlaceLikeOmYoga.com*

For mail orders, please photocopy this form, fill it out, and mail it with payment (in U.S. dollars only) to:

Tandu Publications
428 E. Thunderbird Road #123
Phoenix, AZ 85022

Name _____

Address _____

City_____ State _____ Zip _____

Telephone _____

Email address _____

Direct Order Book price	Quantity	Total
$15.95 per book	_____	$_____
Arizona, add 8.3%		$_____
Shipping in U.S. 1 book $4.00		$_____

For larger or International orders, please contact
via email: *noplacelikeom@hotmail.com.*

Total enclosed $_____